"I have found in my own counse. ... major problem that dominates the lives of too many Christians. It robs them of their joy in Christ and makes them difficult to live around. Dr. Amy Baker has poured into this critical work great wisdom that comes from years of her own personal counseling ministry. Her approach to this destructive problem is refreshingly insightful because she takes the sufficiency of God's Word seriously. Not only does this enable her to unscramble the real problem biblically, but it also enables her to prescribe practical answers with Scriptural insight."

Dr. John D. Street, Chair of the MABC Graduate Program, The Master's College & Seminary; president, the Association of Certified Biblical Counselors (ACBC)

"I've been a pastor and counselor for over twenty-five years now and this is a book I'll be handing out! Christians sing about amazing grace, but too often still live by the law of their own hard work and perfectionistic striving. Amy's done a great job tackling an issue that flies right in the face of the Gospel and God's grace but seldom gets addressed head-on or with the insights that Amy brings to this subject. She exposes not only the hub of the perfectionistic heart, but so many of the related sinful 'spokes' that are connected to this one heart issue—guilt, fear, pride, anxiety, and heightened sensitivity to criticism. And she diagnoses and explains it all so well with practical examples and clear, biblical teaching. Amy doesn't just point out the danger; she shows you where and how to get free and rest in God's grace. This book brings you back to the only perfect person—our Savior, Jesus Christ."

Brad Bigney, MDiv, Pastor, Grace Fellowship in Florence, KY; ACBC certified counselor; author of *Gospel Treason: Betraying the Gospel with Hidden Idols.*

"I counsel, rub shoulders with, and too often resemble Taylor, Ian, Penny, Li ('not satisfied with the way God set up his universe'—ouch!), and the rest of the compelling, real-life situations Amy Baker unpacks.

The tension she addresses is inescapable: God commands perfection but our ongoing sin prevents it. We then respond with anger, frustration, anxiety, and guilt. Without removing this tension, Baker uncovers the heart disorders beneath the many strains of perfectionism and she carefully provides Christ-centered, biblical counsel for each."

Robert D. Jones, MDiv, DMin, Professor, Southeastern Seminary; author of *Uprooting Anger* and *Pursuing Peace*

"If you care about not just *what* your counselees or congregants hear, but also *how* they hear it, this book is for you. With a gracious and encouraging tone, Amy Baker connects and applies the believer's identity in Christ with the empty promises of striving to live by perfect performance. Amy uses personal stories to demonstrate both the practicality and ability of living life in and through the power of the gospel."

Kevin Carson, DMin, Pastor, Sonrise Baptist Church, Ozark, MO; Professor of Biblical Counseling, Baptist Bible College and Theological Seminary, Springfield, MO

"Amy Baker has written a skillful and insightful book to help the perfectionist. Her illustrations are good, and the Scriptures that she uses are practical and powerful. As an exhorter, Amy uses her God-given gift to help turn the perfectionist from self-centered introspection to God-centered praise. I thank God for this book and Amy's heart for God's glory. I look forward to using it in my counseling ministry."

Martha Peace, Biblical Counselor; author of *The Excellent Wife*

"In this book, *Picture Perfect,* Amy has given biblical insight into a form of legalism, self-righteousness, and a performance-based way of living that subtly and perhaps not so subtly turns people away from living in the richness of God's grace through Jesus Christ. And more than that, she has also shown the effects of this attitude on the person and others with whom this person associates. Having done that, she then goes on to prescribe a realistic and very helpful biblical plan for overcoming this self-righteous, performance-based way of living. I already have some people in mind to whom I will recommend this book."

Dr. Wayne Mack, Strengthening Ministries Training Institute, Pretoria, South Africa; pastor/elder of Lynnwood Baptist Church, Pretoria, South Africa

"Amy Baker has written a book that strikes at the root of those of us who still act like we live under the law. Perfectionism is a yoke God never intended for anyone to carry. Amy helps us to see where we have put performance over relationship, where we have tried to prove our worth rather than live under God's amazing grace. I would highly recommend this book for those who don't just need to 'lighten up' but instead are ready to surrender and rest in the perfection of Jesus knowing His yoke is easy and His burden is light."

Garrett Higbee, PsyD, Executive Director of Biblical Soul Care

"I am so thankful that Amy Baker has taken decades of counseling experience and turned it into this wonderfully helpful book. Loaded with Scripture and practical application, this book is just what you need to combat the bitter roots of perfectionism growing in your heart."

Heath Lambert, Executive Director of The Association of Certified Biblical Counselors (formerly, NANC); associate professor of Biblical Counseling at Southern Seminary and Boyce College; author of *Finally Free: Fighting for Purity with the Power of Grace*

Picture Perfect

Picture Perfect

When Life Doesn't Line Up

AMY BAKER

www.newgrowthpress.com

New Growth Press, Greensboro, NC 27404
Copyright © 2014 Amy Baker

Cover Design: Faceout Books, www.faceoutstudio.com
Interior Typesetting and E-book: Lisa Parnell, lparnell.com

ISBN 978-1-939946-37-9 (Print)
ISBN 978-1-939946-38-6 (E-book)

Library of Congress Cataloging-in-Publication Data
Baker, Amy, 1959–
  Picture perfect : when life doesn't line up / author, Amy Baker.
     pages cm
  Includes bibliographical references and index.
  ISBN 978-1-939946-37-9
  1. Perfectionism (Personality trait)—Religious aspects—Christianity. I. Title.
  BV4597.58.P47B35 2014
  248.4—dc23
                                                                2013037870

Printed in the United States of America

21 20 19 18 17 16 15 14   1 2 3 4 5

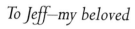

To Jeff—my beloved

Contents

Foreword

Early in my counseling career I had the privilege of working with a young woman whose boss was at his wit's end with my counselee's behavior and was on the cusp of firing her from her job. The problem was—my counselee was obsessed with never making a mistake at work. For example, if she copied something wrong on the copy machine, she would bring the wasted piece of paper back to her desk and stare at it in a trancelike state. She defined a successful day at work as never making a mistake. As you can imagine, she had a lot of bad days. Her boss was a patient enough fellow but he simply could not tolerate a secretary who stared at papers instead of actually doing her job.

At first I thought this woman must be making this up. No one could be that focused on being perfect, could they? As is often the case in counseling however, the more I thought about her situation, the more I began to see ways that I too often focused more on my performance than on the finished work of Christ and my joyful, secure position in Him. I am now convinced that the Lord allowed me to work with that particular perfectionist—my counselee—so I could get a better picture of this particular perfectionist—me.

Amy Baker has done all of us a tremendous service by unpacking this insidious tendency. With love for the Lord and extensive case wisdom,

Amy develops the issue of perfectionism in a way that is winsome, biblically sound, and practically helpful.

I would encourage you to read this book first to counsel yourself and then second to counsel others. It really is true—the best counselor is first a good counselee. If you read these chapters and think you do not need to hear them (i.e., you are perfect), then you probably need to read them again!

This book will help you place less focus on your own righteousness and more on the imputed righteousness of Christ. You will find yourself saying with John the Baptist, "He must increase but I must decrease" (John 3:30). You will also find that the principles in this book really work. Amy is a seasoned counselor and has spent decades working with real-life people struggling with the very issues she is addressing.

I have had the privilege of working with Amy in our church's biblical counseling center for over twenty-five years. Her life is perhaps the best endorsement for the book: she lives and loves Jesus. All of her coworkers consider Amy to be a kind, gracious servant who humbly acknowledges weaknesses as she joyfully rests in the merits of Christ.

By God's grace, my former counselee handled her perfectionism well. Every so often I hear from her and her husband as they update me on what is happening in their life and ministry. It is always such a delight to see her smiling face—a smile that I know comes not from a never-ending pursuit of her own perfection, but in a satisfaction and amazement in the completed perfection of her Savior.

Steve Viars

Introduction

Years ago I heard a woman teaching on perfectionism say something like, "God doesn't expect you to be perfect."When I heard her say that, I was puzzled. I do know that no one is perfect, (Romans 3:10), but there are places in the Bible where God says we should be perfect (Matthew 5:48; 1 Peter 1:16). On the one hand I understood what my teacher meant—that God knows we can't meet his standards on our own, but at the same time, her comment stirred me to study why so many of us are drawn to perfectionism and what God really does expect from us.

I found that understanding perfectionism was far more involved than I had imagined. And, not surprisingly, I also found that I needed to deal with my own heart and life in the unpacking process.

Have I Left Jesus Behind?

Elyse Fitzpatrick asks, "In my pursuit of godliness, have I left Jesus behind? Am I more focused on my performance for him or his for me?"[1] As Christians it's possible to live out our beliefs without a conscious acknowledgment or awareness of his presence. The person and work of the Redeemer becomes secondary to what we're focused on—

living the Christian life. We become primarily focused *on us*—on our performance, our spiritual growth.

I realized how easy it is to focus on "living for Jesus" and think little about what Jesus has done for me. I could get so busy striving for godliness (of course always my own version of "perfect") that I didn't ever think about what Jesus did for me. I was in a race, but I'd forgotten why I was running—love for Jesus.

When that happened, I gave higher priority to my performance and my efforts rather than my relationship with the One who gives me the grace to work. Relationship was minimized; performance was maximized. What I accomplished took on a life of its own, and I was in danger of seeing what I got done, rather than Jesus, as the source of my perfection. I could tell that was true by how I became frustrated and sometimes paralyzed when things didn't turn out the way I expected or wanted. I had to learn and relearn (daily!) that my only perfection is in Christ—in his perfect record applied to my account. Yes, growing in godliness is important, but that growth needs to occur in the context of a relationship that has the right goal and motivation, otherwise my work can't be perfect (no matter how hard I try to micromanage all the details to get things just right) because it's done in my name and for my goals.

Through this process, I have understood more clearly what I need to say to myself and others who are struggling to live the picture-perfect life. I've been reminded that I'm running the race of this life for Jesus and with Jesus. I spent much time thinking about his love that covers over all I do badly and all I do with the wrong motives. I've discovered both how far I fall short and the freedom that comes from trusting in who Christ is and what he has done, instead of who I am and what I have done. That's a weight off my back! I'm hoping that, as you read this book, you will also learn to live in the freedom that comes from faith in Christ. Faith, simply put, is trusting in the work of Another. If you are struggling with perfectionism, I'm guessing it's quite hard for you to trust anyone but yourself. But as you come to Christ by faith, you will find he is absolutely trustworthy. You can give him your whole life, and he will walk with you, give you his Spirit so you can grow more like him, and give you joy as you step into the good works he has prepared in advance for you to do (Ephesians 2:10).

Here's a quick outline of where we are going:

In Part 1, I've described various perfectionists in order to uncover some foundational issues that underlie perfectionism. I've tried to peel back the outer layers of perfectionism to give us a glimpse of what may be happening under the surface of our "picture-perfect" lives.

In Part 2, I've described some key concepts that set the stage for change to take place, including Christ's instruction in the Sermon on the Mount to be perfect as our heavenly Father is perfect. I'll talk about the change process and discuss our satisfaction.

Last, in Part 3, I tackle some of the specific areas that are often troublesome for perfectionists. Things like fear of failure, guilt, pride, criticism, shame, and learning to rest.

Unpacking perfectionism has been a surprising journey that has given me Jesus—and the freedom and joy that comes from walking with him. I hope that you too will learn to walk in freedom with Jesus as your Savior, Brother, and Friend.

Part I

CHAPTER 1

I Love Perfection! I Hate Perfection!

Taylor could feel her frustration level rising. This was the fourth time she had taken the car to the dealership to get the damage corrected. Before purchasing the car, a hailstorm had created multiple dings in the car's surface. As a condition of the sale, the dealership had agreed to remove all the damage at no cost to Taylor. While almost all the dings had been removed, one stubborn ding remained. Taylor had returned the car to the dealership four times now to get it removed. Each time she had brought the car in, the dealership had said they had the problem fixed. Now the service manager was acting like Taylor was making a big deal over nothing.

Taylor's husband told her to quit being so picky. He kindly pointed out that the remaining ding was practically unnoticeable and that the dealership had done a good job on the car. From his perspective, the dealership wasn't obligated to do anything else.

Taylor didn't think she was being too picky. For Taylor, it was simply a matter of doing things right. The car dealership should remove every last ding because they said they would do that for her. And, if they said they would do it, they should. They shouldn't act like it was the customer's fault when they didn't live up to their promise. What was wrong with wanting things done right?

Taylor doesn't just expect this of the car dealership; she expects it of herself as well. She expects to deliver flawlessly when she commits to something. Flawlessly! No shoddy work. No half-finished product. No neglected detail. Picture perfect. If something is worth doing, it's worth doing right. I've been there. Taylor's story could be (and often is) my story. Perhaps you've been there too.

This book is primarily addressed to people like Taylor. People who would in some ways, at some times, and with some people see themselves as perfectionists. Perhaps they don't view themselves as perfectionists in every area and in every relationship, but there's at least one compartment of their lives where perfectionism maps onto their desires and experiences.

Taylor doesn't really think there is anything major about her life that she needs to change. She wishes a whole lot of other people would change. In fact, although she wouldn't say this out loud and may not even realize she feels this way, Taylor wishes others would be more like her. If others would change, life would be better. If the people at the dealership would just be more committed to doing things right (like Taylor) she wouldn't be having this problem. Additionally, if her husband would be the right kind of husband, he would confront the dealership for her and she wouldn't have to keep calling them.

From Taylor's perspective, she cares about doing things right, even perfectly, while others don't seem to have the same commitment. In Taylor's eyes, a whole lot of problems would be solved if other people would just do things right.

Perfectionism's Trademark Characteristics

How about you? You don't have to be exactly like Taylor to have a struggle with perfectionism. Do you want things done right? Does it annoy you that others seem so easily satisfied with what appears to be mediocre performance? Do any of the following "perfectionistic" tendencies resonate with you?

- You want to be the best in everything you do.
- You have very high expectations for yourself and others.
- You are very upset with yourself if you make a mistake.
- You feel guilty for relaxing. You feel like you are never doing enough.
- You're very particular about the details of tasks.
- When you perform well, you analyze your performance for the weak spots and quickly gloss over the things done right.
- You want something done right or not done at all.
- You are perceived by others as a role model.
- You feel like others are never satisfied by your performance.
- You compare yourself to others. If you perceive someone is better than you, you analyze that person to see how to measure up.
- You don't attempt things you know you can't complete with excellence.
- You are frightened by the thought of failure.
- You procrastinate.
- Your relationships are often strained or difficult.
- You feel like you won't ever be perfect.
- You rarely experience joy.

The list identifies some traits that are positive, but it also points out characteristics associated with perfectionism that are clearly troublesome. Traits that make it hard to love God and to love others.

Would it surprise you to learn that Taylor is often frustrated and unhappy? For the last two weeks Taylor has complained to her husband about the car dealership. At work, she has made it clear that she wouldn't encourage anyone to buy a car from this particular dealer. And she has posted a poor review on the dealership's customer review webpage. The dealership gets a one-star rating from her.

A Source of Tension

One barely noticeable ding has become a source of strain in Taylor's relationships. Her high expectations have resulted in conflict. Taylor's relationship with her husband has been strained, even though he only disagreed mildly with her. Taylor got mad because he didn't back her up. She believes her husband ought to support her and take her side on every issue. However, Taylor's husband believes she is unreasonably exacting. Privately, both Taylor and her husband view the other as lacking.

Other people in Taylor's life have had to listen to her complaints. Their concerns have been minimized while Taylor's have been maximized. At the dealership, the service manager has begun to view Taylor as unreasonable. He is no longer interested in keeping her patronage because who wants a customer like her? Who wants to do business with someone who can't be satisfied? The word of mouth that results from customers like Taylor doesn't help, no matter how much they spend on purchases. On the flip side, Taylor isn't interested in giving the dealership her patronage. It's an easily broken relationship, just one of many in Taylor's life—relationships strained or severed because of unmet expectations for perfection. That story has been repeated hundreds of times in Taylor's life. She has wanted things done to a high standard and others haven't delivered.

There is nothing in and of itself wrong with Taylor's desire to have things done right. There's nothing intrinsically wrong with asking dealerships to honor their promise. There's no law against having great-looking landscaping, keeping your car washed and shiny, putting your shoes neatly in the closet, having an organized desk, making sure you always use your blinker when changing lanes, looking your best, living by a strict budget, preparing sharp-looking reports, avoiding junk food, etc., etc., etc. Most people would agree these are good things.

What creates the frustration and unhappiness that comes with perfectionism is what lies under the surface and drives these behaviors— the motives, beliefs, desires, fears, anxieties, and goals that live in and rule the heart and mind. These beliefs and desires interfere with loving relationships with God and others. We'll come back to that later. I think it will make more sense if we first take a look at Taylor's thoughts about her own performance.

The Perfectionist's Self-Assessment

Although Taylor causes stress in everyone around her, what you might not realize is that she too feels unrelenting stress every time she approaches a new task, and she knows she places tremendous pressure on herself to avoid failure. The fear of failure can easily consume her, often causing her to lay awake in bed at night thinking about everything she needs to do so she won't mess up. Her fear of failure often pushes her toward irritability, and those around her would probably describe her as controlling, inflexible, and impatient. But even though Taylor invests heavily in not failing, she rarely feels as though her investment has yielded a high return. When she's done with her latest project, whatever it may be—from cooking dinner for company or launching an initiative at work—Taylor is hardly ever satisfied. For every one thing that went well, Taylor can usually identify twenty things that weren't right. When Taylor perceives she hasn't lived up to the perfection she demands of herself, she then beats herself up as a complete failure and berates herself as a loser who can do nothing right.

Taylor has learned several defensive maneuvers to try to cope with all of this stress. Her fallback strategy is to try harder, believing that more effort will allow her to achieve her goal. But, although she doesn't realize it, this puts her in a repeating loop with no acceptable exit. Her desire to be picture perfect means she is always trying to reach her goal through her performance. When she falls short of the high standards she has erected, she concludes she is a failure and wallows in misery. This ends with a resolve to try harder, greater effort on her part, falling short, more misery, and a renewed resolve to try harder. Because she never reaches the perfection demanded by the performance-driven standards she has erected, she has no way out of the loop other than to quit. Many perfectionists do end up quitting in some, if not all, areas of life. When you can't keep your home as spotless as you would like, you might quit by abandoning chores and allowing things to pile up. If you can't get all "A's" you might just drop out of school. If a job becomes too demanding or you make a mistake at work, quitting might seem like the best option. Or, you may procrastinate on projects out of fear of failure—putting them off because you don't think you can get it exactly right. Taylor however usually just keeps looping back through the cycle.

Another coping mechanism Taylor utilizes is to be incredibly picky about flaws that are quantifiable but to ignore flaws that are harder to quantify. She may insist that the columns in a report be exactly even but not notice that she has driven her personal assistant to tears by making her redo Taylor's project yet again and preventing her from leaving work on time to pick up her child from day care. Taylor is often oblivious to the fact that her relationship with her personal assistant is far from perfect, but she is quick to find typos. Typos and columns are more easily quantified than relationships.

Still another coping mechanism occurs in Taylor's relationships with others. Taylor seeks to control the people in her life so her desire for perfection won't be sabotaged by their mistakes. So Taylor often has rigid rules for others that focus on externals such as performance and appearance. She responds with thinly veiled anger when others fail to follow her rules. When others don't live according to her expectations and it becomes clear she can't exert control over them (as she is finding with the car dealership), she may abandon the relationship or settle for aloof, strained relations. The only relationships she tries to cultivate or foster are with those who seem to be able to accomplish what she desires.

A Distorted Perfection

Yet with all the tension that accompanies her perfectionism, Taylor is reluctant to abandon it. She still desires to be picture perfect. In a distorted sense, Taylor's desire reflects her original purpose. She was created to display "perfection." From the very beginning, God's purpose has been that men and women would reflect his image, that they would radiate the glory of a perfect God, their Creator and Friend. Sadly sin has turned what was once a glorious mission into a source of tension. Sin has also caused us to come up with our own definition of perfection, a man-centered definition that often focuses on performance and outcomes that glorify us, not our Creator.

Why would wanting perfection leave you angry, frustrated, discouraged, or hopeless? The obvious answer would seem to be because others don't share your standard or because you fail to achieve the perfection you desire. But if we go beyond scratching the surface, this answer no longer makes sense.

If we truly valued perfection, we wouldn't quickly become angry and frustrated; those aren't "perfect" responses. Nor would we be controlling, inflexible, and impatient. Those aren't right or perfect responses either. So there's got to be something more going on than simply a desire to do things perfectly.

We've got to start asking questions, "What do I mean by *perfect* or *right*? Why do I want these things done perfectly? What makes perfection important to me? Where does God fit into all of this?" These won't necessarily be easy questions to answer. Uncovering desires can often be difficult. It's also difficult because the answers aren't the same for everyone. But wouldn't you like to be free from nitpicking, paralysis, self-hatred, and irritation? Wouldn't you like to be free to enjoy and accept others even though they don't do everything right? Wouldn't you like to be free to move forward despite your own mistakes and fears of not being right? God can change those things in you, but it doesn't happen by magic. Change begins by looking closely at what is going on under the surface of those feelings and behaviors. It all starts with what we want—our desire life.

Because of sin, good desires become warped and twisted. When you look closely, you can often see that wanting to be excellent doesn't come from a heart that longs to show others the beautiful perfection of God. Instead that desire shrinks and the focus becomes self-centered. You find you want to do all things with excellence because you want others to think highly of you; you want to look good to others or <u>feel</u>

good about yourself. You want to have things under control so that nothing can hurt you.

We can see that in Taylor's life in this way: God has said his two greatest commands are to love him and love others, yet Taylor hasn't really done either in the situation with the ding in her car. She hasn't loved God by trusting him to use even the failures of others for her good. God makes this promise to every believer in Romans 8:28, yet Taylor has functioned as if God can't be trusted to know what is best for her. When he has allowed the car dealership to repeatedly fail to remove the ding, Taylor has responded with anger, frustration, complaining, and impatience.

Nor has Taylor loved others. Instead of patiently and gently seeking to solve problems, Taylor has become increasingly impatient and harsh with the service manager. Instead of building others up in her speech, Taylor has complained. Instead of being kind, tenderhearted, and forgiving, Taylor has nursed a grudge. Instead of extending grace for human limitations, she continues to demand more than they can provide.

Taylor is relying on herself and seeking satisfaction in having things done by her standards (not God's standards). God's desire for Taylor is much different (and so much better) than what she wants for herself. He wants to make her like his beloved Son (Romans 8:29). He wants her to have rich, full relationships where she shares with others the grace and mercy she has been given as a dearly loved child of God. As Taylor begins to understand that the frustration and discomfort in her life comes not from the failures of others or even herself, but from her response to those failures, she can turn to God with her true failure: replacing God at the center of her life with her own desires for perfection and control. As she turns away from her own desires and turns toward God (what the Bible calls repentance), he will begin to help her function as he originally designed humans—to display his image and his glory. This will be a process and there will be many failures along the way, but God will not desert Taylor. When he begins a good work, he carries it on to completion. He will do the same for you.

Exchanging a Heavy Burden for a Light One

Think for a moment now about what you really want on a day-by-day basis. If, like Taylor and me, your heart and mind are often ruled by self-focused desires, it won't be long until you experience frustration, fear of failure, unrelenting pressure, and guilt. It won't be long until you seek to control others to get them to live according to your expectations. It won't be long until you live with a sense of dread that just around the next corner someone will discover you are a fraud; you're not really as put together as everyone believes you are. These are heavy burdens.

Taylor wants things done right because in her heart she believes this will bring her satisfaction. But Taylor has been deceived into believing that the perfection she is seeking will bring happiness. Taylor has been lured into believing that performance leads to perfection and that performance-based perfection leads to happiness and satisfaction. These deceits are advertised regularly by the world around her promoting the perfect body, the perfect diet, the perfect job, the perfect investment, the perfect house, the perfect family, the perfect life. But the reason they resonate with Taylor is that she wants to believe them. She wants to believe that if she works hard enough she can attain perfection. She wants to believe that performing well will remove her anxiety and fear. She wants a life with no hassles or trials, and she believes being perfect will fulfill this desire.

True, there have been brief moments of satisfaction. Occasions of recognition have brought fleeting good moods, but these have inevitably been followed by pressure to do more and fear of being exposed as imperfect. For the perfectionist, achievement results in demands for greater achievement. Not a moment should be wasted in resting on your laurels or celebrating victory. There is always the next game to win, the next project to perform, the next expectation to meet. And the greater the recognition, the greater the fear of being exposed. The more people point to you as a model to follow, the higher the potential for humiliation when you don't live up to the exalted status conferred on you. Perfectionism is a harsh master and serving this master is frightening and exhausting.

A life ruled by our own desires and shaped by what the world tells us is perfection eventually becomes an exhausting life full of disappointment and frustration. In contrast, how radically different it is when the one true Lord rules our lives. When the true Lord rules our lives, we find that his rule is very different. This ruler invites you to come to him and have rest. Listen to his kind invitation in Matthew 11:28–30:

> "Come to me, all you who are weary and burdened, and I will give you rest. Take my yoke upon you and learn from me, for I am gentle and humble in heart, and you will find rest for your souls. For my yoke is easy and my burden is light."

Does this seem attractive to you? Do you feel worn out trying to meet all the demands of perfectionism? Do the anxieties, pressures, and fears that come with perfectionism keep you in turmoil, your mind always churning? Would you enjoy rest for your soul, a relief from the churning?

Jesus promises his yoke is easy, his burden is light. How can he do this? He did it by taking the crushing burden of our failure on himself and inviting us to turn to him in trust and repentance. As we turn to him, he offers us his perfection—his righteous record with no mistakes or flaws. With his perfection as our foundation, he then equips us to live with a whole different mindset. Different things become important to us. We develop different goals and desires. We pursue different agendas.

Be advised, the old desires, fears, anxieties, and goals will still tempt you to rely on them, but in Christ they no longer have the power to rule you. Woohoo! All those tensions that Taylor has lived with for years no longer have to have mastery over her. There can be peace.

Taylor needs a different way. Her striving for perfection has gone badly wrong—led by a heart that has been blinded by the promises of false gods. Her striving for perfection has brought tension into almost all of her relationships. Her striving for perfection has resulted in tremendous pressure to do better and better. Taylor has a love/hate affair with perfectionism, and she needs a better way.

Christ offers a better way. He makes incredible promises that only he can deliver. The life he promotes is radical. It's restful. It's stunningly beautiful. It's the basis for this book.

CHAPTER 2

Ian: Performance-Based Perfection

Ian gazed out the window, not really seeing the lights of the city reflected in the pond his firm had created to beautify their property. Everyone else in the office was gone, leaving him alone to stare out the window and try to figure out what went wrong.

Just yesterday Ian had landed the biggest client his legal firm had ever had. Ian had been courting this client for years. He had worked zealously to prove his firm could achieve better results than any competing firm. For one brief moment, perfectionism had delivered. He felt proud of his success.

Ian had left the office ready to celebrate. He had arrived home to find the house deserted and a letter from his wife on the kitchen counter saying that she was done with their marriage. Ian's stunningly successful day ended with a stunning failure. The envy his colleagues had felt of his success when he left the office will now become scorn, pity, or condescension as news travels through the office grapevine that his wife has gone off with another man, a man much less successful than Ian. The picture-perfect life his colleagues imagined he had will be revealed for what it is, horribly imperfect. Having just scored the biggest triumph of his perfectionism-driven life, Ian has also just experienced an incredible failure that seems to mock his hope of ever succeeding.

Ian goes back and forth between two poles. One pole promises that perfection is attainable if you just work hard enough; if you just push yourself relentlessly, you can have it all. This has often been Ian's guiding star. Captivated by this vision, Ian joined the Marines during college. He wanted to be one of "the few, the proud, the Marines." "Do or die" resonated deeply with him.

With this as his mantra, Ian has often been impatient with anyone who seemed unsure of himself. There is a cockiness to his manner that others tend to interpret as arrogance. He is harsh with those who don't advance with the same bravado he displays. In the Marines, he would openly ridicule others if they evidenced any hesitation during training. Now, as a respected member of the bar, Ian has found more subtle, but equally wounding, ways to express his disdain.

But there is another pole that also seems to have magnetic attraction in Ian's life: shame. While Ian can push himself to success, he also finds failure present in his victories. His biggest successes have often been accompanied by depression. During these times he withdraws, feels anxious and guilty, and questions every aspect of his success. He looks back at all the mistakes he has made and moves whatever victory he may have just experienced to the loss column. When others congratulate him, Ian sees this as evidence that they really don't know him. If they knew him they wouldn't be impressed by his less-than-perfect performance. Ian's conviction that others don't see the true man serves to increase his feelings of loneliness and isolation. Ian feels vulnerable and unsure of himself when drawn by this magnetic pole. He then finds himself responding to others with a gruffness that simply exacerbates the alienation he already experiences in relationships. During these times, Ian has learned to self-medicate with alcohol; he drinks to get some relief from the stress and guilt he carries with him.

Ian's desire for perfection both draws him and repels him. The carrot on the stick dangling before him draws him to perform, but his futile attempts to grasp what seems so tantalizingly close creates frustration and despair. He inevitably winds up feeling empty and worthless as his thoughts circle around and around his failures, eventually prompting him to either try harder to make up for them or numb himself so he can no longer feel their sting.

Ian's problem is not that he desires excellence and perfection. Ian's problem is not that he isn't trying hard enough. Ian's problem is not a sense of inferiority or anxiety. Ian's problem is not even that he has set his standards unrealistically high.

The crux of Ian's problem is that he has set aside worship of the one true God for a god that makes promises that it can't deliver and will never fulfill. Ian worships the god of perfection rather than the perfect God. Ian's god offers itself as a savior from things Ian wants to avoid—anxiety, depression, being seen as inferior by others. Ian's god makes promises that appeal to Ian's pride—the admiration of others, prominence in his social circles, and respect. Ian's god even subtly entices him to believe that God will be pleased if he achieves the performance-based perfection for which he is striving—that Ian's perfection will make God look good. And without realizing it, Ian has embraced this god of perfection.

Do you find yourself standing next to Ian worshipping the god of perfection rather than the perfect God? Do you find it difficult to entrust God with your life—your desires, your hopes, your fears and anxieties? Do you find it hard to believe that God could do a better job with your life than you can, despite evidence to the contrary?

Israel's Story and Ian's Story

The Bible tells a story very similar to Ian's story and perhaps yours as well—it's the story of Israel, the people God called to be his very own. In the book of Deuteronomy, Moses, the man who led them out of slavery in Egypt, reminds them of who they are:

> For you are a people holy to the LORD your God. The LORD your God has chosen you out of all the peoples on the face of the earth to be his people, his treasured possession. (7:6)

Moses explains that God didn't pick Israel because they were "all that and a bag of chips"; God didn't choose them because they were superior or because they were perfect (Deuteronomy 7:7–9). God chose them because he decided to love them. He treasured them.

You might think that being the chosen, the treasured possession of the holy, perfect, and majestic God of the universe and being his visible representation to an imperfect world would create such humility and gratefulness that nothing else could steal the worship of this chosen people. But, like all of us, the Israelites were easily led away to other means of salvation and to putting other gods in the center of their life.

Israel's history is one story after another of leaving the God of the universe for gods they made themselves. But just because they left God didn't mean they didn't want to be righteous. Just as Ian wants perfection, Israel wanted righteousness. And according to Romans 9:31 and 10:2, they were willing to work hard to attain it.

When you think about it, there's really not much difference between a desire for righteousness and a desire for perfection. Righteousness is the quality of being right or just. Perfection represents a completeness and maturity in which any shortcomings or defects have been eliminated or left behind.[2] Israel wanted to be right or just. Ian wants to be perfect.

Israel worked hard to attain their goal, and Ian has worked hard to attain his goal. However, Israel didn't attain the righteousness they pursued; just as Ian has not attained the perfection he has pursued. What went wrong? Why didn't their hard work pay off? Here's how the apostle Paul explains it in Romans 9:32–33 (ESV):

> Why? Because they did not pursue it by faith, but as if it were based on works. They have stumbled over the stumbling stone, as it is written,
> "Behold, I am laying in Zion a stone of stumbling, and a rock of offense; and whoever believes in him will not be put to shame."

Israel failed because they pursued righteousness not by faith but by works. Similarly, Ian has pursued perfection by performance. He has wrongly believed that performing perfectly will bring joy and satisfaction. He has been deceived into thinking that performing perfectly will result in completeness and maturity in which he lacks nothing. Both Ian and Israel desire something good, but both are also missing a crucial component.

Two Desires, Two Failures, One Solution

In Romans 9:33, we read that Israel stumbled and fell over the very person that could make them righteous, Jesus. Ian, too, has stumbled and fallen. Ian has trusted in performance-based perfection rather than relying in faith on a perfect Savior. Because they stumbled over Christ, both Israel and Ian experienced shame. Israel experienced shame for not trusting in Christ for righteousness. They were offered an intimate relationship with God through Christ and the fulfillment of all his promises to them but instead chose a system they thought they could control. Ian has not trusted Christ for righteousness and perfection either. He has depended on his efforts to achieve perfection. Ian lives with the shame of failure; the shame of not achieving the performance-based perfection he desires. Both Israel and Ian know failure. Shame is their companion.

In contrast, Romans 9:33 promises that those who trust in a perfect Savior will never be put to shame. That's an incredible promise. It's a promise perfectionism makes but fails to deliver. Unlike perfectionism, Jesus does deliver. Christ takes our imperfect record—our record of imperfection and shame—and substitutes his own record—a record of perfection. It's an unfair trade. We get Christ's righteousness and perfection on our account; he takes our unrighteousness and imperfection and gets the penalty we should have paid. He takes our shame and gives us hope.

God is faithful, kind, and loving toward us even when we have been disloyal to him. Ian has disloyally chosen to pursue a different savior, the god of perfection rather than the perfect God. He has worshipped being able to perform perfectly and bounced from self-satisfaction when it has seemed within his grasp to anxiety and guilt when he sees his failures and realizes he doesn't measure up. Ian has coveted being one of the few, the proud—both as a Marine and as a civilian—and thus has blindly stumbled into the temple of performance-based perfection. God offers hope to people stumbling blindly in darkness. God offers his perfect Son, the Light of the world.

There is hope for those striving to be picture perfect. People who have stumbled over Christ by trying to attain performance-based perfection find out in Roman 10:9 that if you confess with your mouth, "Jesus is Lord," and believe in your heart that God raised him from the dead, you will be saved. Saved—saved from sin, saved from idolatry, saved from shame, saved from our blind pursuit of something that never delivers on its promises.

While Ian openly or silently condemns those he feels don't measure up, God acts surprisingly different. God is merciful to people who have not measured up; merciful to people who have turned from God toward their own desires; merciful to people whom he created to glorify him but who found the god of perfection more alluring than the perfect God. God sent his Son to open eyes that are blind. The only path Ian has known is trying harder and harder to be perfect. He has stumbled along in his darkness, consoling himself with alcohol when his god disappointed him once again. He has bound himself to a false god. He feels the pain this causes but doesn't realize that he needs a whole new direction; a whole new life.

God provided his perfect Son to become Ian's substitute and to take the penalty for all of Ian's failures—for Ian's less-than-perfect life and for Ian's worship of the god of perfection. Ian deserves death for deserting his Creator, for defecting to the enemy, and worshipping the god of perfection. Death is required, but God's perfect Son can become Ian's substitute. Jesus took Ian's penalty when he died on the cross. All Ian needs to do is to give up his own way, ask for forgiveness for Jesus's sake, and he will have the whole new life he desperately needs.

This is amazing enough on its own, but God did not stop at sacrificing his own Son to die the death deserved by Ian. At the moment Ian believes in Jesus, God will transfer to Ian's account all of Christ's perfection. Christ's perfection will then be on Ian's record. The perfection that Ian can't achieve will show up on his account. Ian will receive a new perfect identity—the identity of Christ.

Christ has purchased a better way for us. He turns our striving to meet the demands of the god of perfection upside down and makes an incredible promise—we can have his perfection. This sounds almost too good to be true, doesn't it? Think about it: Christ has never messed up. Christ has never had to seek refuge in a bottle of alcohol to ease the pressure and dull the guilt and stress. Christ has never looked back at a victory and moved it to the loss column because he found mistakes. Christ is without blemish; he is perfect. Jesus does all things well.

With Christ's perfection as our own, we can begin to worship the perfect God rather than the god of perfection. We can start to love God and others instead of performance and performance-based outcomes. We can start to love perfection simply because it represents Christ and his death in our place, nothing else. We become part of a community whose function is to glorify God and support each other. And to empower us in this, we are gifted with the indwelling of the Holy Spirit. This can change Ian. As we'll see in the next chapter, it can also change Linda, an angry, demanding mother-in-law.

CHAPTER 3

Linda:
The Angry Mother-in-Law

Linda looked over at her daughter-in-law. How could Tony have married this woman? She would never be able to make Tony happy. How could a divorced woman with two undisciplined little girls possibly think she could be a good wife to Linda's son? From Linda's perspective, Tony deserved someone better; and Linda deserved a better daughter-in-law.

During Tony's growing-up years, Linda had worked hard to be a good mother. She hadn't let Tony eat junk food or get hooked on video games. Linda had disciplined Tony and held firm when he threw tantrums and told her she was a mean mom. She hadn't let Tony run with a wild group of kids or date young women without proper supervision. Linda had gone without manicures in order to afford expensive basketball shoes. For Tony's sake, Linda had stayed married to a husband she no longer loved. Linda felt like she had done everything right in bringing up Tony, and she hadn't made all those sacrifices so Tony could marry a girl who'd been pregnant before her first marriage.

Linda was angry at Tony's wife, Linda was angry at Tony, but most of all, Linda was angry at God. Linda had followed the rules. She had been a model mother and this is what she got—a daughter-in-law she was ashamed to be seen with in public.

Linda grew up practicing good works. Even in kindergarten, Linda was pointed out as a role model to others. She had always tried to be a good girl. After graduation from high school, Linda attended college and got a degree in nursing. Later Linda married her college boyfriend and they settled down in the community in which Linda grew up, eventually having a son, Tony.

Linda could be the poster child for a seminar on deportment and etiquette. She carries herself with perfect posture and dresses with fashionable good taste. Linda can host events, dinners, and meetings with charm and ease. Linda can interact with diverse groups of people without blundering. And no one can remember ever seeing Linda commit a social faux pas. Linda has served as the successful chairwoman of local United Way campaigns for years; she teaches a nutrition class at a local women's shelter; and she serves on her church's missions committee.

Linda has gotten so used to being everyone's role model that she has begun to believe that she deserves that position. But, although she looks picture perfect on the outside, her inner person is far from perfect. Under her charming, well-dressed façade, Linda is proud, angry, condemning, and joyless. She has slowly become more and more critical of those around her. For the most part, Linda is silently condemning. She thinks she has covered her dislike for those who don't live by her set of rules with graciousness, but others aren't really fooled. Although they can't single out specific wrong behaviors, they can tell they are held in contempt or dislike. The smile that never seems to reach Linda's eyes, the lack of lingering to chat, the coldness in Linda's demeanor all communicate that others aren't on her level.

Linda thinks she is God's friend and representative, but she has slipped into a life of self-righteousness. Linda's religious life is little more than joyless duty. She goes to church. She reads her Bible and prays but she has no intimacy with the Father and no joy in her relationship with Jesus. Outwardly Linda looks like a dedicated Christian, but the gospel doesn't move Linda. She is trusting in her good works. Because she has worked hard to follow God's law, she has developed the attitude that God owes her. In Linda's eyes, she has earned God's favor and she expects him to bless her demands. But her demands aren't being met. God owes her a daughter-in-law of whom she approves, and he hasn't delivered.

Perfection—Both Inside and Out

Linda correctly understands that God demands perfection to be accepted by him. He is a holy God who cannot tolerate any imperfection or sin. Yet what Linda doesn't seem to have grasped is that this perfection demanded by God is much more rigorous than any sort of perfectionistic standard we can impose on ourselves. Also spoken of as being "righteous," being perfect is more than just doing the right thing, saying the right thing, or looking good according to the standards of our culture. Being perfect includes thinking the right thing and having the right feelings and motives. We aren't perfect if we're nice on the outside while we fume on the inside. We aren't righteous if we give extravagantly to the poor while internally condemning them. We aren't righteous if we dress modestly on the outside while secretly hoping others find us sexy. We aren't perfect if we've earned a bunch of impressive letters to put after our name but haughtily look down our noses at anyone who only has their GED. We aren't perfect if everyone points us out as a role model but internally we think we are better than others. True righteousness is first of all internal before it is external. Being in the grip of pride, anger, or condescension, even if we say and do the right things outwardly, is unrighteous. It means we're not perfect. No wonder Romans 3:10 declares that no one is righteous, not even one.

Mercifully, Jesus came and lived the perfect life we've not been able to live. He successfully met every requirement to be perfect both outwardly and inwardly. He not only performed perfectly, his perfection came from his inner man. He is perfectly loving; he has never been unloving, unkind, impatient, harsh, or mean. He is perfectly humble; he has never been condescending or haughty. Jesus is perfect, both inside and out.

A Foolish Substitute

Linda functions as if her conduct and works give her righteousness and perfection. From there, it's a short distance to being proud when she behaves well and condemning of others who don't meet her standards. Long ago, her husband earned her disdain when he failed to live up to her standards and now her daughter-in-law has also earned Linda's contempt. Linda seeks perfection on her own terms (via a behavioral standard she creates for herself and others) and thinks that God is pleased with her and obligated to her.

Linda is blind to Christ's warning that a focus on appearing perfect to people on the outside can't compensate for an inside that is far from perfect. Linda's contempt for her daughter-in-law, her disdain toward her husband, her superior attitude toward others, and her anger toward God are evidence that Linda's heart is far from perfect.

Linda has a lot in common with a group of people that Jesus had strong words for—the Pharisees. Jesus told these men who focused on outward appearances that they were full of hypocrisy and wickedness. Listen to his admonition in Matthew 23:27–28.

> "Woe to you, teachers of the law and Pharisees, you hypocrites! You are like whitewashed tombs, which look beautiful on the outside but on the inside are full of dead men's bones and everything unclean. In the same way, on the outside you appear to people as righteous but on the inside you are full of hypocrisy and wickedness."

You might think that Jesus's attitude toward the Pharisees (and Linda, who closely resembles them) would reflect the same disdain and contempt that they have shown to others. But even in the midst of his warning, Jesus surprisingly had great compassion. Jesus continued to provide opportunities for them to repent and change. Jesus told them he would send prophets, wise men, and teachers (v. 34), who would proclaim the message of redemption in Christ. Sadly, these Pharisees would reject God's message of mercy extended through these teachers, even killing some of them (v. 34). But Jesus still longed for them to repent. We hear his attitude of compassion in verse 37 of chapter 23.

> "O Jerusalem, Jerusalem, you who kill the prophets and stone those sent to you, how often I have longed to gather your children together, as a hen gathers her chicks under her wings, but you were not willing."

Christ longs for people to come to him for salvation. He is compassionate even toward proud and self-righteous people. Jesus is ready to welcome Linda too, but first Linda has to see that she needs forgiveness and a Savior. Instead she can only see her good works and others' failures (including what she believes are God's failures). She doesn't realize that her anger at God reflects her deep failure to love God and others with her whole heart, mind, and soul.

Although Linda doesn't see herself as rejecting Christ, her focus on her good works communicates a trust in herself that is at odds with the gospel. Linda needs to evaluate whether the salvation she has been trusting in is her good behavior or Jesus. It may be that while Jesus has been Linda's good example, he has not been her Savior. Linda may have used Christ as a role model, but failed to see that she needed him to be her Redeemer. Even though Linda is a leading member of her church, she may not understand that her "good" works are ineffective in bringing her to God. Linda is angry at God, not realizing that in kindness and love, God has been mercifully patient with her. Linda's heart has been full of malice and scorn for others. Her heart is shriveled with pride. God saves us, not because of the righteous things we have done but out of mercy. Linda needs mercy, sadly she doesn't know it. She is actually farther away from God than the daughter-in-law she judges so harshly. Her daughter-in-law knows that she needs Jesus to forgive and help her every day. By contrast, Linda has little of Christ because she doesn't see her need of him.

It's easy to be drawn into the trap of performance-based perfection and to try to achieve perfection by human effort. Instead of humbly receiving the love of our Father and depending daily on him, focusing on him, crying out to him, repenting to him, rejoicing in him, loving him, enjoying his grace, thanking him for salvation, praising him for making us his child, trusting in his forgiveness, and seeking to serve him and others because we are living by faith, we forget the gospel. We focus solely on behavior and we leave out grace. We try to improve ourselves (and of course others). We consciously or unconsciously trust our works to achieve righteousness. But human effort doesn't produce perfection. Our only perfection is in Christ.

Let Go and Let God?

When we understand that our perfection and good works have no power to save us, we may wonder, "Does that mean I just let go and let God?" The answer is an emphatic, Not at all! It was not Linda's good works that created the problem between her and God. It was Linda's heart that was the problem—a heart that took pride in her good behavior, a heart that condemned others for not behaving as well as she perceived she was behaving, a heart that took the position that God was obligated to her because of her good deeds, a heart that loved the approval of others (and really mainly herself!) more than God, a heart that worshipped the god of perfection rather than worshipping the perfect God. Linda needs to cry out to God in repentance to cleanse her heart and then work out her salvation from the cleansed heart God gives, as Paul discusses in Philippians 2:12–13.

> Therefore, my dear friends, as you have always obeyed—not only in my presence, but now much more in my absence—continue to work out your salvation with fear and trembling, for it is God who works in you to will and to act according to his good purpose.

Because of what Jesus has done for you, you do work hard (but not to ensure your salvation—that's a done deal). You "work out your salvation" as one who is so sinful and flawed that you could never get it right on your own and as one who is so loved and accepted that you're 100 percent confident God will help you. Because Jesus has given you a new heart, you have a growing desire to please him in everything that you do. For Jesus's sake, you want to love well and from your heart. You want to extend the mercy and grace you have been given by Jesus to others. You want to live in community with others, not on a pedestal aloof from others. You want to see his kingdom come and his will be done in the world around you. And you are willing to roll up your sleeves and lay down your life for others so God can use you. As you do so, you cry out to God for his grace to teach you how to live a life that glorifies him. You continue to rely on his grace, not your works. You realize your dependence on the Holy Spirit to work in you. When God works in and through your efforts, you are thankful that God has given you the privilege of seeing his kingdom grow.

When you get it right, you don't feel sinful pride; you rejoice that in this moment you have pleased God and thank him for giving you a heart to obey. When you get it wrong, you don't wallow; you repent and rejoice in his grace that offers you forgiveness. When others get it right, you don't envy; you thank God for the gifts he has given them through his grace. When others get it wrong, you don't condemn them or get sinfully angry—you realize they are just as sinful and flawed as you are and you compassionately seek to help them get to a better place by depending on God's grace. You value being part of a community of believers who pray with and for you, provide encouragement and accountability for you, and strive for a common goal—the glory of God.

The Pharisees thought they could become righteous by a system of works. But Christ is the end of works (Romans 10:4). It is through him that there is righteousness for everyone who believes. Linda needs this gospel. Linda needs to stop trusting in her rules of behavior as her source of hope and salvation.

Perhaps you recognize a bit of yourself in Linda. Although she might seem like an extreme example, I know how easy it is for us to struggle with anger toward others who don't measure up and even with anger toward God when life doesn't measure up according to our plans. If you see yourself in Linda, invite another Christian into your private world by asking for prayer. Tell someone who loves God about your disappointment and anger and ask them to pray for you each day for a month.

Perhaps you could even ask several people to do this! Then go to God yourself. Ask for help so that you can love others—even (and especially) those that disappoint you.

In the next chapter you will meet Harmony, a young woman very different from Linda. Harmony grew up with a father a bit like Linda—someone who could never be pleased. Unlike Linda who functions as if her good works put God in her debt, Harmony lives under the burden of believing that God is like her earthly father. Her earthly father was never pleased with her, and Harmony has taken that into her relationship with her heavenly Father. But, just as the gospel of grace, can change Linda, it can also change Harmony.

CHAPTER 4

Harmony: A Daughter Who Is Never Good Enough

Harmony ran her dust cloth over the piano in their living room. She used to love this instrument. Musically gifted, Harmony had begun playing the piano at age four. When she was six, she took part in her first piano competition and came home with top honors.

Piano was more than just an instrument to play sonatas or jazz for Harmony. Piano was the instrument Harmony used to try to win the approval of her dad.

Harmony's dad was also a gifted musician, and many had assumed he would have a career with a well-known symphony orchestra someday. However, backstage politics had resulted in the hiring of a rival musician, and Harmony's dad left the concert hall for good and began teaching private students. Embittered by his experiences as a performer, Harmony's dad became a harsh man. He also became driven to see his daughter succeed; he determined his daughter would become what he had never been, a concert pianist.

At first, Harmony believed she could live up to her dad's expectations. Although he pushed her hard, as she started out, her giftedness made it possible to excel. Harmony's early success led her dad to believe his daughter could fulfill his dreams, and excited by this, he praised

Harmony. When Harmony won a competition, her father would eagerly tell her that now they could start preparing to win a more prestigious competition. But as Harmony began to compete in the more prestigious competitions, the pianists against whom she competed began to match Harmony in ability and skill. When Harmony came away with anything other than first place, she experienced her dad's disapproval.

Extremely sensitive to her dad's displeasure, Harmony devoted herself to her music in order to win her dad's approval. But no matter how hard she worked to meet his expectations, the disapproval from her dad grew stronger and stronger when she failed to win a competition. Harmony wished she could be perfect so her dad would be proud, but she found that no matter how hard she tried, her dad could not be pleased. The piano morphed from being an instrument that brought pleasure to a symbol of not measuring up.

In truth, there is nothing Harmony can do to please her father; she just doesn't realize it. Because of his bitterness, her dad wouldn't be pleased unless the world fell at his feet in admiration that he had sired a daughter whose talent as a musician exceeded that of any human being living or dead (and even that wouldn't satisfy him for long). While Harmony is a victim of his unreasonable expectations, she also wants her father's approval more than anything. Her perfectionism is both a result of her dad's demands and the tool she uses to try to get what she lives for—her dad's approval. Her perfectionism is a heavy burden to her. Instead of centering her life on the perfect God who offers life and rest, Harmony has organized her life around the approval of her father. Her only reward for her loyalty is disappointment and anxiety.

Harmony eventually went to her pastor for advice. At first, she was hoping that he would help her to manage her father's expectations and to help her change the way he treated her. But instead, they started with what she wanted the most in life—the approval of her father. Harmony came to recognize how her heart has craved—even worshipped—the approval of her father. Harmony has spent much of her life trying to please her father and hear his praise, but she is now recognizing that she has loved the approval of her father and lived as if her father was her god.

Impossible to Please?

This is a great beginning, but Harmony has a long way to go to be free from the trap of trying to be perfect. One big thing that keeps tripping her up is her mistaken belief that God is like her father, a parent who is never pleased. Without realizing it, Harmony has put her relationship with God in the same category as her relationship with her father. This has also impacted all of her other relationships. Harmony has a hard time trusting that anyone loves her (let alone God). Friends notice that Harmony is always trying to make them happy, but they also sense a distance in their relationship with her. For her part, Harmony has a difficult time trusting anyone. Not only does she view her relationship with God through the lens of her father's disapproval, she views all other relationships this way as well.

Perhaps you might have done the same thing in your life? Here's how it works for Harmony. She knows that God is holy and perfect in all his ways. She knows that she isn't even close to perfect. To her, it all adds up to never being able to please her heavenly Father. What Harmony has not understood is that God displays his perfection in love and compassion toward her. He is sympathetic to her weaknesses and tenderly reaches out to come to her aid. He tends his flock like a shepherd and carries them close to his heart (Isaiah 40:11). Harmony is precious to her heavenly Father. God is not like Harmony's father, yet Harmony is often convinced that her flaws keep her from God's approval, and she worries that God is never pleased with her. Harmony hasn't given up, she keeps trying, but she misses experiencing the joy available to her in all that she does because she wrongly believes that God doesn't delight in her. How about you? Have you understood that your heavenly Father's love for you is so much better (really more perfect!) than what you might have experienced from your parents? If you grew up with hard-to-please parents, it's easy to get caught in this way of thinking.

Let's examine how Harmony's thinking about God's love has gone in the wrong direction. Harmony is wrong in several ways about God being pleased with her. First, Harmony doesn't understand that when she trusted Christ as her Savior she was placed "in Christ" (Colossians 2:9–12;

3:3). Because she has been given the identity of Christ, when God looks at Harmony, he is pleased because she is in Christ, the Son in whom he is *well* pleased. Next, Harmony also doesn't understand that our ability to please God changes when we are in Christ after salvation. We'll come back to both of these misunderstandings in a minute.

Harmony wrongly assumes God is like her dad. But God is not a bitter old man whose agenda is to see his daughter achieve what he couldn't. God is a loving Father who sent his Son so we don't have to experience the condemnation our sins required (Romans 6:23). Nor is God hoping to achieve glory through the accomplishments of someone else. God is glorious in and of himself, an amazingly perfect Creator to whom all glory, honor, and praise rightfully belongs.

Harmony's conviction that God cannot be pleased is a lie painted to look like the truth. Satan is a deceiver and by taking pieces of truth and distorting them, he can often succeed in fooling us. (Notice how he distorted the truth from the very beginning in the Garden of Eden with Eve.) Let's sort out the truth and the lies with which Harmony and others like her struggle.

A Lie Painted to Look Like the Truth

It is true that no one can earn his or her way to heaven, be holy enough to be acceptable to God by works, or escape God's judgment by living according to a set of rules. It is true that if we kept almost the entire law of God, but stumbled at even one point, we would be condemned (James 2:10). We can never measure up. We will be judged. Prior to salvation, it is impossible to please God (Hebrews 11:6). This is why the lie that we can *never* please God appears to be true. However, it is not true that it is always impossible to please God. This is true only prior to salvation. After salvation, it is *always* possible to please God and to know his pleasure.

Prior to salvation, we had no hope of experiencing God's pleasure. We were simply prisoners waiting our turn before the Judge who would hand down his condemnation and his sentence. We were sinners in the hands of a just Judge. However, at salvation the relationship of prisoner to Judge ends. Christ died once for all and took the full penalty of the sentence demanded by our just Judge. The penalty has been paid, completely and forever. There is no condemnation for those who are in Christ Jesus (Romans 8:1). We are born again, this time as children of God. God becomes our Father. Unlike Facebook, where your relationship status can change with the click of a button, you can never go back to the status of a condemned prisoner after trusting in Christ to be your Lord and Savior.

When our status changes to being a child of God, we can bring God the Father pleasure; much like our children can bring us pleasure. Additionally, God's pleasure is not the result of self-centered motives as it is with Harmony's father. God's pleasure with us, his dearly loved children, is entirely different.

What Pleases God?

Two times while Jesus was living on earth the people around him literally heard God's voice calling out from heaven. What did God say? Did he tell the disciples to keep an eye on Judas because he was stealing from the money pouch? Did he tell the Pharisees they were self-righteous hypocrites? What would prompt God to call from heaven?

God just wanted to say, "I love my Son!" You're probably familiar with the Stevie Wonder song, "I Just Called to Say I Love You." That's what God did. God just called to say, "I love you."

> And a voice from heaven said, "This is my Son, whom I love; with him I am well pleased." (Matthew 3:17)

God publicly announced that he loved his Son. In fact, God is so pleased with his Son that he exalted Christ to the highest place and gave him the name that is above every name. God truly is well pleased with his Son. Furthermore, God is pleased with us when we desire to be just like this Son he adores, this Son who is perfect. It is God's desire for us to be conformed to the image of his Son (Romans 8:29).

The Son is the radiance of God's glory and the exact representation of his being (Hebrews 1:3). Is it any wonder then that God would want all his creation to adore his Son, the Redeemer who was led like a lamb to the slaughter so we could be freed from deceitful desires such as those linked to perfectionism? Christ went to a cruel death on the cross and "God exalted him to the highest place and gave him the name that is above every name, that at the name of Jesus every knee should bow, in heaven and on earth and under the earth, and every tongue confess that Jesus Christ is Lord, to the glory of God the Father" (Philippians 2:9–11). God is well pleased with his Son.

God's Motive for Us to Be Like His Son

Our desire for perfection is generally self-focused. We desire perfection as a means to be accepted or to control our fear of rejection or failure. Like Harmony, our motives for perfection often cluster around a desire for approval or significance. In contrast, God's desire for us to be perfect is just another way of saying, "Worship my Son who has redeemed and rescued you. Worship my Son who suffered a brutal death in your place. Worship my Son who was unwavering in his mission to rescue his own, even when they behaved as his enemies."

In addition to exalting the Son he loves, there is a second reason God wants us to be like his perfect Son. God wants us to look like his Son because he loves *us*. God treasures us; he wants us to have the best.

Why do you teach your children the things you teach them? Because you despise them and their annoying little ways? No, you invest in your children and teach them because you love them. You want to equip them to excel. You want the best for your children. God wants you to look like Jesus because he wants the best for you. There is nothing better than Jesus. God desires you to be like Christ because he loves you.

It's right and proper to long to be like Christ, the perfect Son. *This* perfection is all about Jesus; not about us. *This* perfection is *only* attractive because it represents Christ. We long to be perfected because we want to be conformed to the image of Christ. It comes from a heart that sees Jesus as the greatest treasure one could have.

When we want to be like Jesus, this begins to be reflected in our actions. Our relationships start to change. Instead of spending our time wondering what others think of us and making our goal in relationships to keep others from being mad at us, we begin to genuinely love others instead of fearing them and their disapproval. We begin to seek the good of others, rather than solely our own good. In fact, we begin to consider their interests as more important than our own. And as we do, we start to look more and more like Jesus, our perfect Savior. This is not the product of a heart whose goal is to make us look good or to achieve some self-focused desire. This is the work of God that empowers us to grow in the likeness of Christ and thereby magnify our Savior. And becoming like Jesus pleases God.

Is It Possible to Please God the Father?

As we grow in conformity to Christ, we please God. To review, it is impossible to please God prior to putting your faith in Christ for salvation when the relationship is one of prisoner to Judge. Hebrews 11:6 states it plainly, "And without faith it is impossible to please God." However, after salvation, pleasing God the Father is possible. Through the power of the Holy Spirit, you can always be growing in looking more like Jesus, growing in being conformed to the image of Christ. And as this happens, you please God.

The apostle Paul talks a lot about pleasing God to people who are God's children. And in his discussions, it is clear that he is talking about something that is possible. Let's pause a moment and look at one occasion when Paul did this.

In his letter to people in the church at Thessalonica, Paul tells the Thessalonians,

> Finally, brothers, we instructed you how to live in order to please God, as in fact you are living. Now we ask you and urge you in the Lord Jesus to do this more and more. (1 Thessalonians 4:1)

Notice several points from these two sentences. First, Paul has instructed these believers "how to live in order to please God." It would be senseless for Paul to give these people instructions to do something that is impossible, so we have to infer that it is possible to please God. This is confirmed by Paul's next comment. Paul points out that these people had followed his instructions and were, in fact, pleasing God.

So, while Harmony cannot please her biological father, she can please the Father who has an everlasting love for her. It pleases him when Harmony, through the power of the Holy Spirit working in her, follows the instructions in his Word and grows in Christ's likeness. It pleases God when she desires to glorify him.

Furthermore, unlike Harmony's father who has grown less and less pleased with her, Harmony can please God the Father more and more, just as Paul urges the Thessalonians. As she understands and tastes the goodness of the Lord, she can grow up in her salvation (1 Peter 2:2–3).

Enjoying God's Approval

Harmony's confusion about pleasing God resulted from a lie covered with a patina of truth. It's easy to see why the lie could be convincing. Apart from Christ, we can't please God. But in Christ, with God as our Father and through the power of the Holy Spirit, we can know and enjoy God's pleasure and approval.

Knowing these truths and learning to rely on her heavenly Father's love can strengthen Harmony to turn from her worship of her dad's approval and to worship the one true God and know his approval. As Harmony understands this truth, she can begin to take joy in pleasing God. When Harmony sins against her Father, she can go to him in repentance, receive his forgiveness, and know the joy of a restored relationship with the Father where no grudges are held. When Harmony obeys her Father through God's grace, she can rejoice in knowing her Father is pleased. Harmony's life can become a life of joy.

Now, when Harmony takes a step of obedience, she is learning to say to herself, "By God's grace, because of Christ's sacrifice, through the power of the Holy Spirit, I've taken a step in loving God with all my heart, soul, mind, and strength. Thank you, Lord. Thank you for the grace to take this step in pleasing you."

Living with a bitter old man who can never be satisfied means Harmony's life will never look picture perfect. Unless her dad repents, Harmony's relationship with her father will always involve some degree of suffering. But, as she daily asks for God's grace, Harmony can show kindness to her father even when he expresses his dissatisfaction with her. Sometimes this kindness may take the form of accepting his criticism and making his suggested changes, while at others it may mean confronting his unreasonable standards and refusing to play along. As she does this, Harmony can have confidence that God is pleased. He is pleased that she has honored his Son by following his example of being kind to people who are unkind. He is pleased that by grace she desires to glorify him. He is pleased that she is able to know the joy he gives in difficult circumstances.

Are you like Harmony? Do you spend your life living for the approval of someone significant to you? Or even living for the approval of everyone you meet? You too can learn a whole new way of living. You can step into the freedom and joy there is in worshipping the one true God and desiring to please him. This will gradually, but fundamentally change all of your relationships. As you step away from the burden of trying to make everyone happy, you will be able to truly love others for Jesus's sake. Start by asking God to teach you these truths. Study the passages we went over in this chapter. Ask someone you trust to pray with you about these things.

Remember, because of Christ, you can experience the approval of God. Not because any righteousness of your own has earned you merit or standing before God, but because you are in Christ. Because you are in Christ, Christ works through you and God is pleased with the work of Christ in you. It's amazing to think that although we often can't get the approval of a mere human, it's possible to have the approval of the God of all creation. Such knowledge is almost too wonderful to take in. It is a message of hope for you and all those who have spent their lives striving for approval.

Even more amazing, the hope of the gospel is not just for those who long for the approval of others. It speaks a better word to all kinds of struggles with perfectionism. So it's also a message of hope for those who have given up. Perhaps you are more like Greg, the defeated perfectionist you will meet in the next chapter, and you have just quit trying. Is there also hope for those who are paralyzed by their perfectionism? Yes there is.

Chapter 5

Greg:
The Defeated Perfectionist

Greg doesn't look like what you might consider to be your typical perfectionist. That's because he is a defeated perfectionist. He has tried to do things perfectly, but without much success. Rather than continuing to try, he has given up. Greg works in a low-paying job and hasn't earned any promotions because he does just enough to get by. He looks sloppy, and his apartment is a mess. Every night after work, he goes home and watches TV until he falls asleep in his chair. There is nothing about Greg's current life that would lead you to believe he is striving for perfection.

But of course there is a backstory. Greg grew up with a mom addicted to crack cocaine. To support her habit, Greg's mother turned to prostitution. When Greg was three she began prostituting him to get money for her habit. Defiled by men who had no problem violating a young boy, Greg grew up with shame etched into his soul. This continued until Greg was ten and Child Protective Services stepped in and Greg was sent to live in a foster home. For the first time, Greg had three nutritious meals a day, clean clothes to wear, and someone who cared about his education. Also, for the first time, Greg went to church.

At church Greg heard about God, sin, judgment, Jesus's death on the cross in our place, the gift of eternal life, and a whole new life right now. Greg was encouraged to believe in Jesus. His church also encouraged adherence to a strict set of rules. It was all new to him.

Initially, Greg experienced hope. It seemed he had found a way to remove the shame associated with his background. If he kept the rules, he would be acceptable. So Greg devised a set of rules to live by: he got his hair cut; he started saying "Geez" instead of "Jesus"; he got rid of his "angry music"; and he started going to church every Sunday. Compared to the way he used to look and live, Greg was picture perfect. For a time, the hope of erasing his shame turned Greg into a high achiever. Greg desperately wanted cleansing from the shame attached to his past, and he was willing to work hard to accomplish this.

Greg found that the changes he made didn't erase the shame he carried with him from his past. He trusted perfectionism to protect him from his shame, but he still felt dirty and unacceptable. Greg never felt like he truly measured up in his foster family. He had a sense that he was their project—the poor kid they had rescued and were trying to remodel. Not only that, Greg was still drawn to some of the things he had eliminated from his life in order to live by the rules. He liked hanging out with friends who listened to music that glorified violence and sex, even though he no longer downloaded it onto his iPod. Greg also liked late-night surfing to Internet porn sites even though he felt dirty after doing so. When Greg began dating, it wasn't long before he became sexually active, going as far as his girlfriends would allow.

Greg sometimes wrestled with the thought that he was too dirty and unacceptable for God to help him. He feared God would never bless someone who was drawn to sexual immorality, especially when being abused should have convinced him just how dirty and disgusting sexual immorality was. Yet Greg didn't quit trying to erase his shame through perfectionism.

One night Greg was attacked by a gang because he had started sleeping with a gang member's former girlfriend. Beaten and kicked until he was almost unrecognizable, Greg ended up in the local emergency room, feeling like he might die.

Greg survived the attack, but his perfectionistic striving for the approval of the god of perfection didn't survive. Greg believed the attack was a clear signal that God was displeased with him and that he deserved all the shame and suffering he received. So Greg quit trying. He quit trying to live up to the perfectionistic rules he thought would cause him to merit God's help and approval. His sleeping around proved he couldn't do it. Although Greg recovered from the physical wounds he received, he didn't recover from his desire to be picture perfect. He still believed in the god of perfection, but because of his many failures, Greg gave up trying to achieve in order to demonstrate that he was really an acceptable person. Perfectionism still has a death grip on his heart, but now he uses apathy as a shield against the shame he continues to feel.

No More Shame

Shame, disgrace, suffering. Greg feels alone and separated from others because of these. His alienation is heightened by the fact that the promise held out by the god of perfection—the promise to remove his shame—has been proved false. Perfectionism didn't deliver, and it left hopelessness in its place.

Greg has confused the god of perfection with the one true and perfect God. The god of perfection has no power to remove shame or help the needy when they suffer. The god of perfection insists that those who worship it remove their own shame. The god of perfection draws people into deeper despair.

Greg has failed to understand that he will never be able to remove his shame by living a perfect life. Sin and shame (our own sin and shame or the shame resulting from the sin of others against us) stain our soul so indelibly that our efforts to wash it away are completely ineffective.

An old hymn asks, "What can wash away our sins?" The answer: nothing but the blood of Jesus. Then the hymn writer asks, "What can make us whole again?" The answer: nothing but the blood of Jesus. Notice how the hymn writer builds on this theme as the hymn continues.

Refrain
> Oh! precious is the flow
> That makes me white as snow;
> No other fount I know,
> Nothing but the blood of Jesus.

> For my pardon, this I see,
> Nothing but the blood of Jesus;
> For my cleansing this my plea,
> Nothing but the blood of Jesus.

Refrain

> Nothing can for sin atone,
> Nothing but the blood of Jesus;
> Naught of good that I have done,
> Nothing but the blood of Jesus.

Refrain

> This is all my hope and peace,
> Nothing but the blood of Jesus;
> This is all my righteousness,
> Nothing but the blood of Jesus.[3]

Refrain

When we understand this, the idea of Jesus's blood cleansing us from all unrighteousness takes on a much richer meaning. Greg is right to recognize that his efforts can't remove his shame. But Greg has not understood that the blood of Jesus purifies us from all sin. Jesus is able to cleanse us from all unrighteousness.

We're reminded of this in 1 John 1:7, 9.

> . . . the blood of Jesus, his Son, purifies us from all sin. If we confess our sins, he is faithful and just and will forgive us our sins and purify us from all unrighteousness.

While the context indicates that this passage is primarily referring to sins we commit, we cannot dismiss the fact that Jesus has the ability to purify us from *all* sins, including sins committed against us, which have stained and defiled[4] our souls.[5] In their book *Death by Love,* Mark Driscoll and Gerry Breshears put it this way, "On the cross, Jesus dealt with the sin that has stained your soul. Jesus both forgave your sins at the cross and cleanses you from all sins that you have committed and that have been committed against you."[6]

Greg didn't understand that Jesus came to take Greg's shame on himself. When Isaiah says that God's servant, Jesus Christ, took up *our* infirmities and carried *our* sorrows (see Isaiah 52:13–Isaiah 53), he is saying that Jesus took Greg's shame on himself. Jesus was humiliated in degrading ways just as Greg has been. Jesus was publicly stripped naked and tormented. He was defiled. He was beaten beyond recognition. Jesus endured the cross and its shame, but shame didn't become his focus (Hebrews 12:2). Jesus's focus remained steadfastly on his Father and on our healing (1 Peter 2:23–24).

When Christ purifies us from all unrighteousness, he substitutes his righteousness for our shame. Instead of shame, we get Christ's perfection, his righteousness, on our account. We own it.

Defeated perfectionists like Greg especially need to understand that they are now entitled to the privileges that come with Christ's righteousness. If you have trusted Christ, you have been gifted with Christ's righteousness and you are entitled to the privileges that come with righteousness. So, let the passages that follow nourish your soul. Meditate on the fact that if you have trusted Christ as your Savior these promises are for you.

Gifts and Privileges for Those Who Have the Righteousness of Christ on Their Account

God upholds the righteous (Psalm 37:17).

If you've trusted in Christ, his identity has been substituted for yours. You are righteous. Therefore God upholds *you*! He supports you. He backs you up. He champions you and endorses you. God is not upholding you because you've earned it or met a certain benchmark of your own making. He upholds you because you have the righteousness of Christ. You have God the Son's identity so you can trust that God will not snatch this privilege away from you (Romans 4:24; 5:17; 1 Corinthians 1:30; 2 Corinthians 5:21).

God blesses the way of the righteous, he surrounds them with favor as with a shield (Psalm 5:12).

God blesses you! He surrounds you with favor *as with a shield*. Like Greg, you may have used perfectionism as a shield against suffering and shame. How much more joy would it bring you to have God's favor as your shield? At salvation, God began a good work in you and he won't abandon you. Any direction you look, you are surrounded on all sides with help, with God's largesse, with his good will and backing. Because you have the identity of his Son, God surrounds you with favor. Nothing can provide greater hope and protection than this!

God delivers the righteous from troubles (Psalm 34:19).

Although you may have many troubles and afflictions, God will deliver you. He will rescue you; he will free you; he will relieve you because you have the righteousness of Christ. It may look different from what you hoped or expected, but God's deliverance runs deep and redeems completely.

Even when you fall, God will enable you to get back up. The righteous falls seven times, but he rises again (Proverbs 24:16).

You can overcome failures because of God's grace. Even when it seems as if others are determined to sabotage you, God will enable you to keep going and prosper. When you fail, God will come to you in grace and help you up.

God listens for the cries of the righteous (Psalm 34:15).

The Lord not only hears us, but he is listening out for our cries. His ears are attentive. You may have felt that you have no right to speak and/or expect to be heard since you have not achieved perfection, but, in fact, God is listening for you to cry out to him. What an important gift and privilege of the righteous.

The prospect of the righteous is joy (Proverbs 10:28).

You can move forward without shame. Your prospect is joy. The forecast for your future is bright.

The Cross Reassures Us

It requires grace to believe these gifts for the righteous apply to you because sometimes it seems like we're not delivered from troubles, that our way is not blessed, that we aren't flourishing, that we've fallen. We don't have health and wealth and others may actively despise us. We still feel dirty.

Consider the cross. On the cross it appeared that Christ was not being delivered from troubles, that his way was not blessed, that he was defeated. His prayer to have the cup taken from him seemed to have been ignored. He cried out, "Why have you forsaken me?" It appeared he had lost everything. But God took what appeared to be defeat and made it the means of rescue for all mankind. We are saved through what looked like total defeat.

If God could do that with the cross of Christ, do you believe he could take what appear to be defeats in your life and turn them into victories? Do you believe that in all things God works for the good of those who love him? This may be difficult to believe. Follow Christ's example from the cross and keep entrusting yourself to the Father (1 Peter 2:23). Then you can respond in faith to seeming defeat. As this happens, you won't wallow in your failure, you won't fret over it, and you won't complain. Instead, you determine to trust God.

It may be that you've fallen and experienced defeat because you temporarily stopped trusting in God. You turned back to your own way. You've sinned. But, by God's grace you can turn to him and ask for forgiveness. The Bible calls this repentance. If your defeat is due to sin on your part, you can ask God's forgiveness and trust that he is as merciful as he says he is and that he delights in forgiving you. If what seems like defeat was not due to sin on your part, wait patiently, trusting that God is up to something you can't fully see.

Remind yourself of the truth from God's Word: *Even though it appears that I've failed, I know that what looks like a failure, will still be used by God for my good and his glory. Nothing can separate me from my Father's love* (Romans 8:28–39). The cross looked like a failure for God, but it was the means that God used to save his people from sin and death. Remember that in God's world how things appear is not how they really are. Behind the most disappointing circumstances stands the love of the Father, the sacrifice of the Son, and the gift of the Holy Spirit. God holds all things in his hands and works all things for the good of those who love him.

Up to this point, Greg has felt shut out from God and others because of his shame. He has quit in many areas of life because he has felt like it didn't matter what he did. He has given up on genuine relationships. But if Greg trusts in Christ's blood and Christ becomes his substitute, Greg has a new life and new reason to live. In Christ, all things become new.

The writer of "Nothing but the Blood" ends his hymn on this note of triumph:

> Now by this I'll overcome—
> Nothing but the blood of Jesus,
> Now by this I'll reach my home—
> Nothing but the blood of Jesus.
>
> Glory! Glory! This I sing—
> Nothing but the blood of Jesus,
> All my praise for this I bring—
> Nothing but the blood of Jesus.

CHAPTER 6

Penny: Living for Jesus?

Penny grew up in a two-parent home with parents who loved the Lord and sought to follow him and love others. Penny's mom was a stay-at-home mother who devoted herself to her family. Her mom was up before six every morning fixing a hot breakfast for Penny, her dad, and Penny's older brother, Paul. French toast, hash browns, oatmeal with brown sugar and raisins—these were some of the smells that drew Penny out of bed in the morning. Penny's mom didn't even buy cold cereal. Penny's dad was a faithful husband and father, and at his job he was known for his integrity and work ethic. While not perfect, Penny's parents were kind people who were sincere in their love for the Lord.

Penny's mom enthusiastically threw herself into her children's education. She volunteered at the school twice a week and made sure the kids always had their homework done. "Work before play" was the motto Penny's mom would often recite when the kids wanted to play before doing their homework. Penny's mom also helped organize other areas of the children's lives. Beds were to be made before breakfast each morning, toys were to be put away before getting out other toys, and clothes for the next school day were always selected the night before.

Each night in family devotions, the children would rehearse their Sunday school memory verse so they would be able to recite it perfectly to their teacher the following Sunday. Sundays were the most important day of the week. Dressed in her Sunday best, with Bible in hand, Penny and her family sat in the fourth pew from the front at church. Her parents always chose this pew saying that being close to the front cut down on distractions. At lunch, the discussion always included what they had learned that morning.

When Penny was eleven years old, she stole a candy bar from a gas station while her dad was filling the tank of the family van with gas. After eating the candy in secret, Penny became fearful that the police were going to come and arrest her. She became jittery when someone came to the door, and she didn't want to go outside and play in case the police drove by and recognized her. Guilt colored her entire world. Her dad noticed that something was wrong and drew her aside to chat about what was troubling her. Penny wept as she confessed her theft to her dad. Drawing her into his arms, Penny's dad explained the Father's love and the Son's sacrifice and that night Penny trusted in Christ, asked him to forgive her for her sin and rebellion against him, and became God's child. Penny was so thankful that she was forgiven by God and cleansed from her sin that she was filled with enthusiasm to live her life for God. She studied her Bible eagerly so she could get to know better this God to whom she belonged.

When Penny grew older, got married, and began her own family, she wanted to replicate the home in which she had grown up. Her childhood was happy, and she wanted that for her children as well. Penny wanted to provide a perfect upbringing for her children. Over time, some of the things she used to enjoy in her relationship with the Lord lost their significance. After being up half the night with a colicky baby, Penny's study of God's Word before breakfast became a duty, and she found herself watching the clock so that she could close her Bible and move on to other things. Gradually study became a duty even if she had managed to get a good night's sleep; she hurried to get through her devotions so that she could fix a hot breakfast for her family.

During church, instead of eagerly worshipping and concentrating on the teaching, Penny often found herself distracted by keeping the children under control. Why wasn't Jake standing up to sing? Where did

Oliver get that red marker? Why was Erin turned around looking at the people in the row behind her?

Penny wants her family to know the Lord and to live life for him, and she is serious about pursuing godliness. But something is missing. Her Christian life sometimes looks more like a pursuit of a picture-perfect family than a relationship with Christ. Penny often evaluates her success by how obedient her children are, how orderly her home is, whether she has read her Bible and prayed each day, and whether her husband is pleased. Somewhere along the line, the gospel of grace was put on the shelf. Penny's purpose became oriented around living a godly life and bringing up godly children. The gospel became past history.

Past History or Current Events?

As I mentioned earlier, I've found it is easy to focus on "living for Jesus" and think little about what Jesus has done for me. My goal has become warped. Perhaps you've noticed the same thing in your life. Perhaps you're so busy striving for perfection you don't ever think about what Jesus did for you. Like Penny and me, you're busy doing things that look very godly but you do them from a heart that is focused on yourself. You're in a race in which you've forgotten why you're running—love for Jesus.

When this happens we develop habits that put the focus on our performance and our efforts rather than our relationship with the One who gives us the grace to work. Relationship is minimized; performance is maximized. What we do takes on a life of its own and we start to see our accomplishments, rather than Jesus, as the source of our perfection. That's why you and I both need the gospel today. We need a Savior today. It is by grace we have been saved and we continue to desperately need grace (Ephesians 2:8–9). We need grace now.[7] Our only perfection is in Christ—in his perfect record applied to our account. Yes, working to grow in godliness is important, but the work needs to occur in the context of a relationship that has a proper goal and proper motivation, otherwise the work is ultimately for us and about us—we have put ourselves in the center of our world, instead of God.

This does not mean we add another layer of perfectionism that applies to our hearts and motivations (e.g., my obedience is not good enough until I really *feel* it). Rather, it means that we work toward an obedience that flows more and more from a heart that is growing progressively toward a greater love for God and others and that is driven by an increasing personal knowledge of Christ. God is pleased with us as we *continue* to open our hearts to him in relationship and allow him to transform us into the image of Jesus. For those who are compelled by a relationship of love, there is a delight in the deeds, a joy in pleasing the Father, a great sense of awe in being allowed to love others like the Son has loved us, a gladness in radiating the glory of the Son.

We Need a Relationship of Love and Grace

It's impossible to have a relationship with the god of perfection. You can't have a genuine relationship with something that isn't alive. When we live for the god of perfection, our lives will be oriented around tasks and performance and appearances. These will be a burden to us and eventually become meaningless.

God invites us into a relationship of love and grace. He can't wait to show us the immeasurable riches of his grace in kindness toward us in Christ Jesus. It gives him great pleasure to come alongside us and help us. So, when we walk through deep waters, he will be with us. And he won't be with us just as a supportive friend who goes with us to the doctor's office when we're being biopsied for cancer. That alone would be significant, but there is more than that in this relationship. God goes with us as a friend who has the power to control outcomes and who cares enough to permit only that which can deepen our relationship, our intimacy, and our reflection of his love and character. He gives grace.

It is grace that trains us how to live godly lives done from a heart that loves God, not a system of rules we impose on ourselves to become perfect. It is the grace of God that teaches us to renounce ungodliness and worldly passions, and love for him that makes us want to. It is love for God that causes us to desire his grace to live self-controlled, upright, and godly lives. It is not our system of rules for perfection (Titus 2:11–13). (And if it is grace that accomplishes these things in us, it would be wrong to take personal credit for them when they occur. The right response would be to praise God for his love for us.)

We all fall short, desperately short. We all need grace. We need a Savior who not only rescues us from eternal condemnation but who helps us in our daily lives. Apart from him we can do nothing. We need to cry out to God to help us in our weakness. We need the help of the Holy Spirit living in us. We need grace to come to Christ in faith for salvation, and we need grace to conform to Christ after salvation. We're not any more capable of achieving righteousness or perfection on our own after salvation than we were prior to salvation. We need God's love and grace for everything in our lives. Penny has this in common with Ian, Linda, Greg, and Harmony.

We're a Lot Like Each Other

At first glance it would seem that Penny has little else in common with Ian, Greg, Linda, and Harmony. An outside observer probably would not describe Penny as driven by deceitful desires and idols (like Ian), as self-righteous (like Linda), as living for her parent's approval (like Harmony), or as someone who has lived with shame (like Greg).

The ambition that seemed to be obvious in Ian seems to be completely missing in Penny. But is it? Is her heart never drawn toward being the best? Does the pleasure she experiences when people praise her children never tempt her toward pride and put pressure on her to make sure her children measure up? In fact, Penny is much more like Ian than it seems.

By looking closely at Penny's heart, it's also possible to find self-righteousness. The self-righteousness in Penny is more subtle than the self-righteousness in Linda. Penny sometimes follows the Lord wholeheartedly and consciously obeys from a heart of love that is dependent on his grace. At other times she trusts in her performance; she leans toward believing that unless she parents perfectly, her children won't come to know the Lord. And sometimes, like all of us, Penny's motivations are a mixed bag.

The shame that led to perfectionism in Greg is also harder to see in Penny but nevertheless it influences her life. In junior high, one of the boys in Penny's class backed her against a locker and groped her before school. While several of the boy's friends stood snickering, Penny fled to the restroom in tears. Penny never told anyone what happened, but the embarrassment and shame of that moment remains firmly etched in her memory. She still vividly remembers how it felt and the laughter of the other boys. While far from the shame and uncleanness Greg has experienced, nevertheless Penny struggles with thoughts of her shame. To overcome the memories, Penny is drawn toward making her surroundings as clean and perfect as possible. Perhaps if she can keep her surroundings perfectly clean, she won't feel dirty.

Finally, the misunderstanding that so clearly led Harmony to conclude that she could never please God has surfaced in Penny as well. After growing up with a mother who lived by the motto, *work before play*, Penny feels like God is displeased whenever she relaxes because there is always more work to be done. She also feels guilty when she feeds her family cold cereal, certain that God is displeased that she didn't fix a hot breakfast.

This is a nuanced discussion. The self-righteousness that was easy to see in Linda is harder to see in people like Penny. What was obvious in Ian, Greg, and Harmony is not as readily identifiable in Penny. Penny seems to have many dimensions to her perfectionism. This can make it harder to see her heart and understand her underlying motives. It can also be hard to see in ourselves. It can be hard to know whether our motives are pure or polluted, self-centered or God-centered. Like the psalmist, we need to ask the Lord to search us and know us and to see where we are going wrong (Psalm 139:23–24).

Our perception of ourselves can frequently be inaccurate. Our minds are deceitful (Jeremiah 17:9), and we tend to believe the best about ourselves (Proverbs 16:2) rather than seeing the things we have made more important than God. However hard this may be, it is crucially important. If you don't see how wrong you are, you won't understand how great the gospel is. If you aren't a sinner, then you don't need a Savior. The grace, restoration, reconciliation, forgiveness, mercy, patience, power, healing, and hope of the gospel are for sinners. They are only meaningful if you admit that you have the disease and realize that it is terminal.[8]

John Calvin has pointed out that human hearts are factories of idols.[9] We can pump out new gods to worship at tremendous speed, even though we often fall back on our old favorites. We all have things we desire and love with more fervor and allegiance than the Savior. We all have desires that we will sin to get or sin when we don't get them. We all have other gods that we trust and fear, deceits that we meditate on, and corrupted desires that we believe can bring us satisfaction. The apostle Paul described his struggle in this way:

> So I find this law at work: When I want to do good, evil is right there with me. For in my inner being I delight in God's law; but I see another law at work in the members of my body, waging war against the law of my mind and making me a prisoner of the law of sin at work within my members. What a wretched man I am! Who will rescue me from this body of death? (Romans 7:21–24)

All who know the Lord battle with a war raging inside them. The environment contributes to the war: the sins of others against us; the influence of a culture that believes happiness can be found in the right dress size, the corner office, or athletic skill; and/or the praise of others. All these and more interact with our desires in the war to make us a prisoner of sin. We all need to be rescued. Who can and will rescue us? Paul went on to answer his own question.

> Thanks be to God—through Jesus Christ our Lord! So then, I myself in my mind am a slave to God's law, but in the sinful nature a slave to the law of sin. Therefore, there is now no condemnation for those who are in Christ Jesus, because through Christ Jesus the law of the Spirit of life set me free from the law of sin and death. (Romans 7:25–8:2)

As Paul continues in chapter 8, he describes priceless treasures given to those who have been freed from condemnation.

- You are loved and accepted.
- You are God's heir.
- You are redeemed.
- You are chosen.
- You are forgiven.
- You are empowered.
- You don't have to pay the price for your sin.
- You will never be separated from God's love.

Paul's answer points us to our position in Christ and also to God's plan to conform us to Christ's image. Paul reminds us that we are saints for whom there is no condemnation, even in the midst of describing his suffering as a sinner who needs to repent. Thanks be to God who has rescued us through our Lord Jesus Christ!

We're All Multifaceted

While we may see one aspect of perfectionism—for example, self-righteousness or shame— standing out more boldly than others among those who struggle with perfectionism, in reality we're all multifaceted. Ian, Greg, Harmony, and Linda are not one-dimensional any more than Penny. Humans are complex creatures. All who belong to the Lord are a mixture of saint, sufferer, and sinner.[10] However, in these cases and the cases that follow, I've tried to make it easier to address certain perfectionistic struggles by highlighting various facets of the person's struggles. Nevertheless, if you were to meet these people on the street you probably wouldn't see this picture. You'd probably see someone who seems a lot like you—because in many ways all of us are like the rest of us. We're creatures designed to reflect a high, holy God who are drawn to other forms of worship by the world, the flesh, and the devil.

While there are unique features to every individual's story, this doesn't negate God's design of humans in his image and our turning aside to worship something other than the one true God. It doesn't nullify the rescuing power of our great Savior and it doesn't alter the process the Holy Spirit uses to bring about biblical change. The process of change described in Part 2 is for all of us. And for all of us change happens as we learn to live out of the good news of all that Christ has done for us and in us.

Part 2

CHAPTER 7

A Perfect Standard

As Trent was growing up, it soon became apparent that he was both academically and athletically gifted. Teachers and coaches loved him because he worked hard and excelled in both his studies and sports. He was a model student and a leader in his chosen sports of basketball and soccer. Trent was an obedient son and made his parents proud. Yet Trent was rarely satisfied. Any grade below an A was unacceptable in his mind, and if he missed a shot in basketball or a goal in soccer, he would beat himself up for days even if his team won.

Now, as a forty-year-old man, Trent has risen to the top of his profession but he has left behind a string of broken relationships, all destroyed by his critical demands of others and unwillingness to show grace. People don't enjoy being around him. The closer the relationship the more true this seems to be. Trent's kids avoid him when they can or keep their heads low when they can't; his wife secretly can't stand to be around him. Trent is every bit as critical and hard on himself as he is with others—no flaw goes unnoticed and mistakes result in mental scourging. Trent is driven to achieve a picture-perfect life, but life never seems to line up that way.

While Trent can see that something needs to be changed, he has no idea what to do. While he can see every flaw in his performance, his heart remains a mystery to him. He is unwilling to lower his standards, but the tension created in his relationships and the pressure he puts on himself to meet his standards is almost unbearable. Many people have told Trent to quit being perfectionistic, to chill out and relax, but to Trent this is meaningless advice. What does it mean to quit being perfectionistic? Quit striving for perfection? Then strive for what instead? Excellence? Who defines that? How do you tell when you're there? Trent sought out Mike for advice because Mike seems different than other men Trent has known.

Change Your Standard

Even though Trent asked Mike for advice, he was pretty sure he knew what Mike would tell him. As they sat in Starbucks having coffee, Trent braced himself for what he thought Mike would say, telling himself, "Here it comes, it seems like all the advice given to me is that I have to just change my unrealistic, unreachable expectations. You're about to tell me to lower my expectations. I've heard that over and over and it doesn't help or make sense to me."

But that was not the advice Mike gave Trent. Mike did not tell Trent to lower his standards. Surprisingly Mike said that God sets the bar higher than even Trent does. Mike told Trent, "In Matthew 5:48 Christ gives the evaluation standard you're to use: 'Be perfect as your heavenly Father is perfect.'"

When Mike said this, Trent threw his hands in the air. "How's that supposed to work? I'm already stressed out and now I have to be as perfect as God!"

God's Standard

"Be perfect as your heavenly Father is perfect." This instruction to those listening to the Sermon on the Mount (Matthew 5—7) and to us when we read it seems to make the bar impossibly high.

Jesus had been leading up to this already in his sermon. Jesus told his listeners, "You have heard that it was said to the people long ago, 'Do not murder, and anyone who murders will be subject to judgment'" (Matthew 5:21). Undoubtedly his Jewish listeners had heard that before. It was one of the Ten Commandments, so of course they were aware of the law against murder. Few perfectionists hearing this statement would have been uneasy, this was a command that they believed they could keep.

But Jesus raised the bar by telling his listeners that getting sinfully angry with someone or calling someone a fool was off limits. So, it's not acceptable to get off the phone with an incompetent customer service rep and mutter, "Idiot"? It's not acceptable to respond to the driver who cuts you off by grinding out, "You fool, what are you doing!" as you slam on the brakes? Perfectionists often feel as if they are surrounded by folks who just don't get it, people who have to be given instructions more than once, people who don't meet deadlines, people who just don't seem to care. Fools. Idiots. As Jesus raised the bar on this issue, the perfectionists in the audience must have started to feel anxious.

Next Jesus reminded his listeners of the commandment forbidding adultery. Again, his Jewish listeners were well aware of this commandment and again most perfectionists hearing this would probably have considered this a law they could succeed at keeping. No sleeping around. No hooking up. Got it. But Jesus didn't stop there; he once more raised the standard by telling his listeners not to even look at someone lustfully. No second look at the woman with the low-cut top. No commentary on the personal trainer with the washboard abs. No wondering if she or he thinks you're hot. For the perfectionists, the stress level went up again.

Then Jesus went on to raise the bar on the subjects of divorce, promises, getting even, friends, and enemies. The stress must have become crushing as the perfectionists heard all these high standards. As the crowning summary of what he had been saying, Jesus concisely stated, "Be perfect, therefore, as your heavenly Father is perfect." This was the knockout blow. Any perfectionist hearing this must have been shattered.

The Blessing of Having a Perfect Standard

Jesus didn't give the command to be perfect as a curse. He gave it as a blessing. Like Trent, you may be wondering, *Seriously? How is this a blessing?!*

God gives us the standard of perfection to drive us to him. This standard helps us see how desperately we need him. We just can't meet this standard. The bar is too high; it's an impossible dream.

John MacArthur makes these observations:

> The sum of all that Jesus teaches in the Sermon on the Mount—in fact, the sum of all he teaches in Scripture—is in these words ["Be perfect, therefore, as your heavenly Father is perfect"]. The great purpose of salvation, the goal of the gospel, and the great yearning of the heart of God is for all men to become like him. . . .
>
> That perfection is also utterly impossible in man's own power. . . . Man's own righteousness is possible, but is so imperfect that it is worthless; God's righteousness is impossible for the very reason that it is perfect. But the impossible righteousness becomes possible for those who trust in Jesus Christ, because he gives them his righteousness.
>
> That is precisely our Lord's point in all these illustrations and in the whole sermon—to lead his audience to an overpowering sense of spiritual bankruptcy, to a "beatitude attitude" that shows them their need of a Savior, an enabler who alone can empower them to meet God's standard of perfection.[11]

Christ has done what we can't. He met the standard. Christ came and lived the perfect life we've failed to live. When Jesus raised the bar, he knew what he was doing. He knew we would never be able to meet the standard. He wanted to show us our need for him. He wanted to be our perfection.

We know that God cannot tolerate sin in his presence, but equally true is the fact that sin cannot tolerate being in God's presence. We often fail to be moved by what Jesus has done for us because we don't want to see how much more perfect and glorious his life is than ours.

That would mean having to sacrifice the perfect system we've created that promises us safety, comfort, and superiority. But when we see the beauty of the life Christ lived, we are forced to admit that our "perfections" are not so very great after all.

Trent has been trying to live according to a standard he has created, but it is a standard that focuses primarily on himself. As far as human standards go, Trent's are very high—higher than the standards of many others. Trent has done many things with seeming perfection and has risen to the top of his profession, but as MacArthur says, Trent's perfection is so imperfect that it is actually worthless.

Why doesn't Trent's hard work add up to perfection in God's view? The problem is that Trent's desire for perfection comes from a heart that longs to be satisfied and sufficient in himself. Trent has missed that God's perfection demands love—a love for God and a love for people. That's a standard that all of Trent's efforts haven't even scratched the surface of. Sadly, the people in his life would say that Trent has failed badly at loving them. Trent is worshipping the god of perfection and he wants to be that god. In the process he is ignoring God's call to love him with his heart, soul, and mind and his neighbor as himself. Not only has Trent missed the mark with his own efforts, but he has been using the wrong standard of perfection all along—his own.

As Mike discussed these things with Trent and his words sunk in, Trent felt broken. But broken is not a bad place to be. Christ said, "Blessed are the poor in spirit, for theirs is the kingdom of heaven. Blessed are those who mourn, for they will be comforted" (Matthew 5:3–4). Broken can be a good thing.

Broken is a very good thing if it drives us to God, if it causes us to cry out to Jesus in repentance and trust and receive the gift of his perfection. Once we get to this place of despair, we're in a place to welcome the perfection of Christ. Now it's good to hear, "Be perfect as your heavenly Father is perfect," because this is our gift in Christ Jesus. Christ has not given us some second-rate perfection, slightly used and defective. Christ has gifted us with the very perfection of God. The perfection of the one to and about whom the seraphim cry out, "Holy, holy, holy is the Lord. The whole earth is full of his glory." Christ has gifted us with the perfection of the One who is not just better than others, but absolutely perfect with no defects, blemishes, or imperfections. Flawless. This is the perfection we get in Christ. Amazing! Amazing and humbling. We don't deserve a gift like this. We're not worthy. We're mortal. Yet this gift is given to all who trust in Jesus.

As a result we can never be satisfied with lesser standards of perfection. Our standard of perfection now changes to become the standard of our holy and loving God. Our one desire becomes to be like Christ in our day to day living because we have this great gift. Our ideas about perfection also begin to change. We begin to see perfection both as a *gift* that Christ has purchased for us and as a *process* of growing in Christlikeness. Once a source of stress or despair, perfection becomes a wonderful goal. Because of the gift we've received, we want to live a life of love (Ephesians 5:2) because that's what our Savior did. Being perfect as our heavenly Father is perfect will mean we want to love God with all our heart, mind, soul, and strength and love others more than ourselves—exactly like Jesus did.

A Perfection from the Inside Out

Christ's Sermon on the Mount also made it clear that genuine perfection (the perfection of God) is first and most importantly internal, not external. The Sermon on the Mount demands not just that people *do* right but that they *be* right. Christ makes this clear near the end of the sermon with an illustration of a tree and its fruit. Christ said, "Every good tree bears good fruit, but a bad tree bears bad fruit. A good tree cannot bear bad fruit, and a bad tree cannot bear good fruit" (Matthew 7:17–18).

The only way to have good fruit is to have a good tree. You have to *be* right. A bad tree cannot bear good fruit. Whereas the perfectionists in Christ's audience may have been willing to settle for some sort of external "perfection"—fruit that came from a bad tree but looked edible—Christ demolishes external perfection. He warns against people who look good externally but are corrupt internally (wolves in sheep's clothing according to Matthew 7). Perfection must come from the deepest recesses of the heart. Again, this standard is a bar too high to reach.

Trent may have risen to the top of his profession, but thus far his success seems to be the fruit of a bad tree, as evidenced by his string of broken relationships, his critical demands of others, and his unwillingness to show grace. It is much easier for Trent to appear "perfect" in the big moments of life than in mundane situations. You can see from his impatience in the fast-food line, his irritability when people are late, his harsh comments to his staff, and his stern approach to his wife and children that Trent has not been living a life of love. Instead he's been living a life of selfish ambition, which is the antithesis of how Christ lived and calls us to live (Philippians 2). What has been going on in his heart?

Underlying Trent's drive for perfection (and our own!) is a heart of unbelief. Trent doesn't really believe that God will provide for him; and so he has trusted in himself for security. That's why it's so important to Trent that there be no errors in his work or flaws in his product— he's afraid people won't accept errors or flaws, and he will be ruined because of their rejection and the financial loss associated with their rejection. In Trent's belief system, when other people make mistakes, they need to be brought back into line by whatever methods work so that their mistakes can't harm him. This path of unbelief has resulted in fearful selfish ambition. Since Trent isn't confident God will provide, he feels as if he must look out for himself.

But Trent is not an orphan who must fend for himself. As God's heir, God promises that he will supply all of Trent's needs according to his glorious riches in Christ Jesus. More than just material needs, God will supply Trent with the power and ability to love and obey him and to love others more than himself. Trent must develop a habit of choosing to believe God.

As Trent has wrestled with believing God will supply all of his needs, he has uncovered a new facet of his struggle. Trent is willing to believe that God will meet his needs but he is afraid God may not provide as abundantly as he wants. Trent is afraid that his income will decrease, and, though his "needs" may be met, he will have to live on less. Trent is reluctant to have this happen, so it is tempting to keep practicing his old habits. At the root of this is a heart that fears suffering.

In seeing that he is broken, without any possibility of living the perfect life of love, Trent has made a great start. But now he needs to learn how, with the help of the Holy Spirit, to apply God's gift of perfection to his daily life. How does knowing that we have Christ's perfection, in place of our own imperfections help Trent? How does it help you and me? Can that simple truth really change our relationships and how we treat people? The next chapter will guide you into living out who you already are in Christ.

CHAPTER 8

Growing into Our Position

Over the history of the world, there have been times when rulers became kings or queens while they were still children. For example, Louis XIV of France became king at age 4, King Tut of Egypt at age 10, King Josiah of Israel at age 8, Henry VI of England at 9 months old, and Mary Queen of Scots became queen at 6 days old. Of course, at such young ages, these rulers weren't ready to rule. They needed to be educated in order to rule with maturity and wisdom (although this didn't necessarily mean they did rule with maturity and wisdom). Most likely these children would have had a royal education in history, diplomacy, war, the arts, religion, and other subjects thought necessary for ruling well.

When God gives us the gift of salvation, we become royalty. Our Father is the King, the supreme, perfect ruler of all creation. Like these child rulers however, although we retain the position of royalty, we're not prepared to reign practically. We need a royal education.

Child rulers like Louis XIV, Tut, Josiah, and others illustrate the difference between our position as one who has trusted in Christ for salvation and our current abilities. Our position is one of a full heir of God. We have all the perfection of Christ. We have no mistakes, failures, or blemishes on our account. On the royal documents in heaven, we have all the righteousness and perfection of Christ. We are royal heirs.

However, like these child rulers, practically speaking we're far from ready to assume our position. We need to be trained. We need to grow to be like Christ. We need training in God's royal academy.

As Mike and Trent discussed the concept of a royal education, Trent felt like a kindergartner on the first day of school. He did want to respond in love and gratitude to the love he had received from his Father. He was eager to grow in godliness (1 Timothy 6:11), to be conformed to the image of his brother Christ (Romans 8:29), to glorify God in all he did (1 Corinthians 10:31), to put off his former self and put on the new self (Ephesians 4:22–24), and to take up his cross daily (Luke 9:23). He wanted to learn all of these things (and this was very new for him), but for the first time in his life, he also knew that he was just a beginner in God's school.

Growing Up

God designed for us to begin our life in him as infants (Mark 10:15). God wants us to *grow up* into our position as his heir (Ephesians 4:15). God wants us to grow in the royal attributes fitting for kings and queens (Ephesians 4:1–13). God's grace trains us in the royal trait of godliness (1 Timothy 4:7). God's grace works in us as we work out our salvation (Philippians 2:12–13).

Trent has worked hard to be perfect, but he has worked at all of the wrong things. Now he is beginning to learn to come to his Father in heaven as a dependent child, looking to him to supply all he needs for growth in Christ's likeness. Trent is just learning God's patience and gentleness. Trent is just learning God's delight in him. Trent is just learning to forsake his trust in himself for perfection and security.

How about you? Have you learned these essential lessons? Or is your perfectionism getting in the way of being truly perfect like your Father in heaven? What happened in Trent's life can happen to you as well. You can ask your heavenly Father to forgive you for Jesus's sake. You can come to him as a little child and ask for help to be like him.

We will never be able to perfectly fill our royal shoes until we are with God in heaven. We will be students in God's royal school for the rest of our lives on earth. There are lessons Trent will need to learn as he grows up. Trent can't skip school, nor can we. We all need to grow. Trent will not be free of failures. He will mess up regularly and we will too. As Trent proceeds through the royal academy, he will need to regularly remind himself that God wants him to come as a child who is dependent on his grace and love . . . *and that this is a good thing.*

Perfectionism had locked Trent into a painful cycle of trusting in himself for everything and constantly fearing he would be ruined. As a dependent child of God, Trent no longer has to carry the weight of the world on his own shoulders. You also no longer have to carry the weight of the world on your shoulders. You have a heavenly Father who loves you, a Savior who died for you, and the Spirit of God who is at work in you. You are free to work for God's glory while trusting God with the results.

You will notice that it is easy to slip back into old ways, but that doesn't mean you should quit school. Simply turn again to your heavenly Father who will love and forgive you. You can always go to him in repentance, ask for forgiveness, and then rest and rejoice in God's help. God will give you a new desire to love him and others. It's okay that you will have many opportunities to repent and turn again to God in faith. This is what it means to live out your royal education—not as someone who has it all together, but as a little child that needs constant help from our heavenly Father.

This might still seem a bit abstract to you. So let's look together at how living as a dependent child in God's school can change how we view and respond to suffering.

Suffering

Trent devoted much of his adult life to avoiding suffering. He used achievement to try to protect himself from hardship, and he was intolerant of anyone whose errors or failures put him in jeopardy of experiencing suffering.

When Trent was seventeen years old, his father declared bankruptcy. His father had started his own business and used all the family's assets to get the business up and running. But after two years, the company still wasn't breaking even, and with a family to feed and care for, Trent's dad was reluctantly forced into bankruptcy.

Forced to sell everything, Trent's family moved into a one-bedroom apartment, where Trent and his brother Randy slept in the living room, taking turns sleeping on the floor or the couch. All the money the family had hoped to use to send Trent to the college of his choice was gone, and even with scholarships, there was no way Trent could afford to attend the college he wanted. Trent's only choice was to attend a two-year community college, live at home, and get a job to pay for his tuition. Trent felt a profound humiliation at his high school graduation when he rose to give his speech as valedictorian and a PowerPoint showed that his future plans were to attend a two-year college. Of course a two-year college was a great choice, but not in Trent's mind!

Suffering engulfs those it inhabits. Pain seeks to smother joy and crush its victims. Without God's help, suffering can control its victims for life, as it seems to be doing with Trent. The psalmists plead, "Come quickly to me, O God, I am in desperate need" (Psalms 22:19; 31:2; 38:22; 40:13; 70:1, 5; 71:12; 79:8; 141:1). We hear those cries and recognize them in our own groaning.

It's completely understandable that not just Trent, but all of us try to avoid suffering. Yet God tells us two surprising things. The first is that his Son was made perfect in suffering. Can that be true? Christ was made perfect through suffering. Wasn't he already perfect? This seems too hard to understand. Nevertheless, Hebrews 2:10 reports that the founder of our salvation was made perfect through suffering.

John Piper explains, "Suffering deepens faith and holiness. The process through which Christ demonstrated deeper and deeper obedience was the process of suffering."[12] In his humanity, even Jesus himself experienced perfection as a process, not of removing sin (because he had none) but of having his human nature refined even more into the perfect image of God that humanity was designed to be, even in the face of suffering and death. In suffering, we are given the same opportunity as Christ to demonstrate deeper and deeper obedience to God. We are given the opportunity to grow into the likeness of our Savior and to develop a more deeply intimate relationship with him by sharing in his sufferings (Philippians 3:7–11).

God wants to use suffering as part of the process to change us. So we grow in faith and love—a child of God and heir of the King who is worthy of the title. Romans 8:17 explains that as God's heir, we are called to share in Christ's sufferings as a prerequisite to sharing in his glory. This is a hard truth, but it is also so comforting. The prospect of sharing in Christ's glory can keep us from being overwhelmed because we know suffering will not have the final word in our lives. Like Jesus, we may experience great pain and heartache in this life, but because of Jesus, our suffering now serves a greater purpose that is for our good rather than our harm.

For Trent and for us, the process is unimaginably hard, yet God's second surprising instruction is that we are to consider it pure joy when we face suffering (James 1:2–4). Trent's response upon learning this was incredulity. "Seriously? Pure joy. How could I possibly consider something that crushes me as pure joy?" The answer given in James 1 is simply this: suffering becomes our opportunity to become mature and complete, fit to rule. As we persevere in suffering, we find that we grow in faith and love and gradually leave behind desires not worthy of rulers. The joy comes not in the painful trial we experience, but as we see what God does in and through us as we face those trials by faith.

Suffering has the power to expose us. The humiliation Trent experienced as he got up to read his graduation speech revealed how much he wanted to be highly regarded by others; his desire to avoid any whiff of failure; his fear of suffering. These were desires Trent was largely unaware of. Yet suffering revealed that in the deep recesses of Trent's heart, he craved the high regard of others and feared adversity.

Suffering uncovers the secret passions of our hearts that have been hidden not only from others but ourselves as well. Pain can reveal the hidden desires of our hearts that so often spin out of control: our devotion to self-righteousness, our desire for comfort, our passion for the approval of others. Exposed by suffering, it becomes clear these desires have no power to help us. They're impotent, unable to rescue us from disgrace, unable to shield us from shame. They are unmasked as worthless, and we feel stripped naked.

Surprisingly God comes near in our suffering. He sees the shame of our nakedness and, rather than sneering and mocking, he clothes us—he removes our shame and disgrace and clothes us in royal robes. He gives us his glory.

As Trent has been exposed to this new way of thinking about suffering, he is beginning to understand why those who trust in God will not be disappointed. God doesn't laugh at your shame, he doesn't stand in the crowd and ridicule your nakedness; he removes the disgrace of his people from all the earth. Not by waving a magic wand, but by transferring it to the One who was shamed on our account. God shows us love.

God's love coming to us in our suffering changes the meaning and interpretation of life and the universe around us. Rulers need clear discernment and suffering brings clarity to the world. Human passions and intrigues lose their power when one has suffered as God's heir. Suffering brings sense to your world by directing you to what is truly valuable, your Savior.

As the suffering process progresses, you learn to love God more deeply. You learn to cry out, to cling, to trust. You cry out as the psalmists did. "Hasten, Oh God to save me; O LORD, come quickly to help me" (Psalm 70:1). "Be my rock of refuge, to which I can always go; give the command to save me, for you are my rock and my fortress. Deliver me, O my God" (Psalm 71:3–4). "Be not far from me, O God; come quickly, O my God, to help me" (Psalm 71:12). You cry out like Jesus did with loud cries and tears. You want God to hear. You long for his help.

When Trent was seventeen, he didn't know to cry out for help to the Lord. All he knew was the humiliation of his suffering. Trent is in a different place now. Trent has trusted in Christ to be his Lord and Savior. Trent is an heir of God. Now, by God's grace Trent can cry out to God to help him in his unbelief. He can ask God to strengthen him to truly believe that his riches in Christ Jesus are better than the riches of material wealth.

Hebrews 5:7 tells us Jesus's cries were heard because of his reverent submission. Trent can show reverent submission as he battles with his fear of suffering. Having lived through the bankruptcy of his father's business, he never wanted to return to that place in his life. Fighting this fear is painful but profitable. Trent can live out his faith by clinging to God and his ways and repenting of allowing his fear of hardship to control him.

Trent can demonstrate his growing trust in God with a deeper obedience to God's way of love. He can show God's love by speaking gently to his staff and his family when they mess up. Rather than trying to get people back into line as quickly as possible so that their mistakes can't ruin him (one of his reasons for using harsh words), Trent can depend on the Holy Spirit's power and treat others tenderly instead of harshly and impatiently. This will require deep trust on Trent's part because he fears treating people gently won't produce the results he has always longed for in the past.

When his fears are strong, it will be tempting for Trent to stop clinging to God and to reach for one of the plentiful idols making false promises that he won't have to suffer. Of course he will be tempted to return to his old habits of trusting in himself and fearing financial ruin. Trent's old perfectionistic habits will call loudly, inviting him to turn and cling to them. His old way of thinking will lure him with the lie that if he can just do things perfectly, he won't suffer. Perfectionistic thinking baits you, but it doesn't deliver. Now is Trent's opportunity to trust, to believe God's Word when he wants to turn away. Now is Trent's opportunity to show his loyalty to his Savior. This is Trent's opportunity to believe that Christ really is *the* way, *the* truth, and *the* life; he is not a dead end, a liar, or a murderer.

While my circumstances look different than Trent's, I find I need these truths even more desperately than Trent. I too need to cry out for God's help in my weakness. I too need to be reminded that my idols are worthless. How about you? What is God teaching you in his school about yourself and your need for Christ as you go through suffering?

The One we love became a man of suffering. He was despised and rejected. He was crushed for our sins. He finished his work so that the holy God of the universe could welcome sinners into his presence. Know that your suffering will end. It will end in inexpressible, overflowing joy; it will end in glory and honor for the One you love; and it will end in the embrace of your Savior and Bridegroom.

CHAPTER 9

More Classes in God's Academy

Trent's director of operations buzzed and asked if he could have a few minutes of his time. When he arrived in Trent's office he said he had some bad news. Their biggest customer was pulling his business and going to a competitor. Coupled with a seasonal drop in sales, this meant the company would be looking at significant losses over the next quarter.

Trent immediately felt a rush of anxiety about the future. Memories of his father's bankruptcy crowded into his mind. The next three days were extremely unpleasant for everyone around Trent. His employees were harshly scolded for even the tiniest error, his family was lectured about their laziness and careless spending habits, and even the dog was roughly pushed aside when it tried to lay its head on Trent's knee.

On the fourth day, as Trent was reading in Isaiah, he came to Isaiah 26:3–4.

> You will keep in perfect peace
>   him whose mind is steadfast,
>   because he trusts in you.
> Trust in the LORD forever,
>   for the LORD, the LORD, is the Rock eternal.

Although Trent had read this chapter in Isaiah before, on this particular morning it had a powerful impact on him. Trent realized that he had forsaken his trust in the Lord and gone back to depending on himself. He didn't have peace and he was controlled by anxiety. As he considered this, Trent's upside-down world began to turn upright again.

Trent went to God in humble repentance for his distrust of God's goodness. He confessed to God that once again he was believing that material riches could provide security. He asked for forgiveness for not believing that it was God (and not his company) that would abundantly supply all his needs. Then he went to his family and coworkers and asked forgiveness from them as well.

The word *repent* means to change your mind or purpose, so it will probably not surprise you that Trent wants to change. He wants to go in a different direction. His old way of life has become distasteful. Trent wants to be different because he loves the One who first loved him. God has been opening Trent's heart and he has begun to see the hope in Christ, the riches of his inheritance as God's child, and God's great power at work in him.

As Trent has been rooted and established in God's love, he wants to be an imitator of God. Because he is God's dearly loved child, he wants to live a life of love.

Discipline and Growth

God is at work in Trent's life to produce changes in him. God is also at work in your life to produce change in you. God wants you to continue to mature and to put on the graces befitting an heir. He is orchestrating your education (including the difficulties you are facing right now) so that you can grow up to look like his Son whom he loves—God wants the image of Christ the King to radiate from you.

You might have already noticed that the maturing process is sometimes awkward and sometimes it seems to stall. But God's work in us will not be stopped. He will complete his good work in you and me. As we grow, we will become aware of more ways that we need to grow.

We will become sensitive to more sins—more ways we fail to love God and the people around us—and our continuing need for forgiveness and grace. Like young children learning to rule, we need instruction, perseverance, humility, and discipline. It's hard to be a beginner. We would all like (especially those of us who struggle with perfectionism) to perform competently and skillfully from the start. Yet God's method for his children reaching maturity has always been growth—a slow process that occurs one tottering step at a time.

God's plan is for us to *grow* in the grace and knowledge of our Lord and Savior Jesus Christ (2 Peter 3:18). God plans for us to assume in daily life all Christ's character and righteousness that has been attributed to us because of Christ's work on our behalf. God desires his image to be reflected in us and that beauty is perfected through growth. Ephesians 4:22–24 explains the growth process this way:

> You were taught, with regard to your former way of life, to put off your old self, which is being corrupted by its deceitful desires; to be made new in the attitude of your minds; and to put on the new self, created to be like God in true righteousness and holiness.

In this passage growth involves three steps: (1) we are to put off our old self, corrupted by deceitful desires; (2) we are to change our thinking; and (3) we are to put on our new self, taking daily steps in practicing true righteousness.

To put off our old self, God calls to us to strip off our "deceitful desires." Take a moment to reflect and think what might be your "deceitful desires." Trent needed to strip off a desire to achieve security through self-effort; a desire to control life by performance-based perfection; a desire to be thought of as perfect rather than to point toward our supremely perfect Lord; a desire to be independent and self-sufficient rather than dependent on the all-powerful God. What about you? Can you identify the desires that God is calling you to leave behind?

And then there are all the actions that flow from what we want. We also need to put off all the behaviors that are fueled by our wrong desires. Disrobe. Put off your old self. This starts with the simple act of turning to God and away from our sins.

We also need a new attitude. This is a critical component in the process. We have to practice a new way of thinking. Instead of spending our time thinking about how to get what we want, we need to dwell on God's promises to supply all of our needs according to his glorious riches in Christ Jesus (Philippians 4:19). We need to remember that God will not only supply all of our material needs, he will supply joy, encouragement, faith, and peace. God will supply according to his glorious riches in Christ Jesus.

God is not limiting his supply only to our perceived needs; he will supply *according to his glorious riches*. There is a difference; our needs are far smaller than God's riches. Thus, if God supplies according to his glorious riches, we can expect to be lavishly and abundantly supplied—beyond what we could ask or imagine.

Do you see how putting off our old desires and thinking about God's riches will change the way we think about others? Rather than viewing others as tools to advance our agenda or as hindrances to our agenda, we think of others in a renewed way. We see others as fellow heirs of God or as persons living in darkness in need of grace and mercy. Condemnation toward others can be replaced with humility; superiority toward others can be replaced with gratitude for God's grace.

Of course, we will be tempted to return to old habits of thinking. I struggle with old ways of thinking every day. And it's easy to slip back into self-focused thoughts of either worry or pride, but with God's rich help, we can begin to take our thoughts captive and bring them into obedience to Christ. We can be renewed in the spirit of his mind.

"Put on the new self, created to be like God in true righteousness and holiness." In addition to renewing our minds, God calls us to renew how we treat others—how we act like God. We bring Christ to those around us in what we say and in what we do.

It takes practice to put on our new self. We are called to grow in the *grace* of our Lord Jesus Christ; this favor from God; this *charis*, this gift. Grace is the soil that nourishes our growth. It is in God's favor and loving-kindness that we grow. And because of that favor and loving-kindness, we search his Word to know his character, to find out what pleases him, and to make sense of the world.

From God's Word we learn to add to our "faith, goodness; and to goodness, knowledge; and to knowledge, self-control; and to self-control, perseverance; and to perseverance, godliness; and to godliness, brotherly kindness; and to brotherly kindness, love" (2 Peter 1:4–9). It's not all up to us to learn these things though. Peter starts this section by reminding us that God's power has given us everything we need for life and godliness (2 Peter 1:3). But, as we depend on God for help, we also think carefully and specifically about how to grow in all of these areas. Our desire for the wrong kind of perfection has led us to think and act in specific ways, so also our new desire to perfectly love God and others leads us to think and act in new ways.

For example, Trent can begin to think about and treat his children differently. In the past, although he has loved his children, he has been hard on them. He hasn't treated them as souls to nurture and bring up. He has expected them to toe the line so he won't suffer. Because of the love and security he is receiving through Christ, Trent wants to show love to his children. He wants to make specific plans to show his renewed mind in his speech and actions. Therefore, he decided to put off always giving his children commands and sending them off to do what he directed. Instead of giving them hard-to-keep commands, Trent has decided to daily help his children do what he asks. So, if he instructs his daughter to help carry the dinner dishes from the table to the kitchen, he will help too. If he asks his son to pick up his toys, he will help him put the toys in the toy box. Trent will do this at least once daily for each of his children. When they finish, he will hug the children. Just as Trent sinned against his children in specific ways, growing in grace means that now he thinks about how to bless his children in specific ways. This is a practical way we can learn to live out our identity as heirs of our heavenly Father. How about you? What are some specific things you can put off? What are some specific things you want the Spirit to help you put on?

As we grow we often falter—and even feel like we are going backward instead of forward. I've seen this over and over again in my walk with the Lord. But God's love enables those who have the righteousness of Christ to repent and turn back to God again and again. At times it may seem like one step forward and two steps back, but God's grace enables those who have the righteousness of Christ to keep trying—again and again. At times it may seem as if a stubborn desire will never be conquered, but God's strength empowers weak people to put life-dominating sins behind them through step-by-step growth (1 Corinthians 6:11–12).

This growing, this rising and falling, will be painful. The process requires discipline, and no discipline, whether self-imposed or laid upon us by God and others, seems pleasant at the time. It's hard to be a beginner. It's painful to allow others to see our fumbles; it's painful to realize we've gone back to desires and habits we desperately wanted to put off. Yet our perseverance will lead to a good end—a harvest of righteousness and peace.

So don't quit! Pray for God's help. Ask others to pray with you as well. Look for accountability and support from your Christian community. As you learn the lessons of suffering and growth, you will be equipped to excel in a third course designed for heirs to the King. You are invited to enter his courts with praise (Psalm 100:4).

Praise and Thanksgiving

Rulers, dignitaries, and those receiving honor enter palaces and parliaments with well-planned pomp and circumstance. They are schooled in the appropriate etiquette for their entry. Likewise, in God's school, we learn the appropriate way for a royal heir to enter God's courts. As rulers who will regularly enter God's courts, it is good to understand proper court behavior. We are to enter God's courts with thanksgiving and praise.

This course in the royal academy may well become your favorite. You will get to do what you are made to do—worship God. This always turns our world right side up as we meditate on our God and what he has done and is doing in the world.

In five short verses in Psalm 100 we have the course text for praise and thanksgiving.

> Shout for joy to the LORD, all the earth.
>> Worship the LORD with gladness;
>> come before him with joyful songs.
> Know that the LORD is God.
>> It is he who made us, and we are his;
>> we are his people, the sheep of his pasture.
> Enter his gates with thanksgiving
>> and his courts with praise;
>> give thanks to him and praise his name.
> For the LORD is good and his love endures forever;
>> his faithfulness continues through all generations. (vv. 1–5)

First we learn how to enter the royal courts. We are to enter his gates with thanksgiving and his courts with praise. We get to be noisy when we come; we shout for joy (Psalm 100:1). We are to give thanks to him and praise his name (Psalm 100:4).

We are to come before him with joyful songs (Psalm 100:2). We can do this because the Lord is God. It is he who made us and we are his, we are his people, the sheep of his pasture (Psalm 100:3). We can praise God because he is good and his love endures forever (Psalm 100:5).

Throughout God's Word we see that God's heirs regularly practiced this. Praise flowed from them in celebration, in suffering, in fear and anxiety, when persecuted, when sick, in daily routines such as meals, when criticized, and when betrayed.

Trent is not used to praise on such a grand scale, nor are we. We experience disappointment and suffering that suck the life from us. We find anxiety and stress thrust on us with a brutality that leaves us breathless. And praise can be hard to find in these moments.

Yet praise can permeate even these moments. In *31 Days of Praise* Ruth Myers states, "[The command to give thanks] does not mean you should deny your negative thoughts and feelings and attitudes, sweeping them under some inner emotional rug. It doesn't mean you should repress them into some deep cavern where, again and again, they can sneak back into your thoughts, press you into unwise choices, and filter past your defenses to pollute the emotional atmosphere around you."[13] The psalmists didn't do this, nor should you. Nevertheless, the psalmists routinely praised in the midst of their lament. Listen to the psalmist as he begins Psalm 108.

> My heart is steadfast, O God;
> I will sing and make music with all my soul.
> Awake, harp and lyre!
> I will awaken the dawn.
> I will praise you, O LORD, among the nations;
> I will sing of you among the peoples.
> For great is your love, higher than the heavens;
> your faithfulness reaches to the skies.
> Be exalted, O God, above the heavens,
> and let your glory be over all the earth. (vv. 1–5)

Reading this, we would naturally conclude the psalmist must be prospering. Things must be going well for him. But as we continue we learn in verse 6, this psalmist is in danger. He is in trouble. We now hear him pleading for God's help, asking God to grant him help against the foe (Psalm 108:12)—pleading for God to give victory over the enemy's armies.

So we too must learn to intertwine praise with our pleas for help. We must learn to express our confidence in our Father as we wrestle with the armies we face—armies of fear, stress, frustration, self-righteousness, exasperation, anger, and failure. "For the LORD is good and his love endures forever; his faithfulness continues through all generations" (Psalm 100:5).

Progress in God's Academy

As you progress through these courses in God's academy you would be wise to look back occasionally. When you do, more than likely you'll find that as you've cried out to God for his help so that you can learn new habits—habits of faith, love, and godliness—God has powerfully answered your prayer with more grace and maturity; you're growing up into your royal shoes. Growth has occurred one step at a time as God's grace has enabled you to head toward your goal to be like Jesus. Taking one step at a time has meant you've moved on from the place you started and have reached a new place. In this new place you'll see fresh truths about God and about yourself. Certainly you'll see setbacks, times when you retreated to the false gods of self-righteousness, fear of man, or surface perfection. Growth is often like climbing a mountain trail full of switchbacks.

Nevertheless, God's promise that when he begins a good work he carries it through to completion (Philippians 1:6), should be clearly visible in your backward gaze. You realize that maturity has begun to be reflected in your approach to life. You're not an infant anymore. The resemblance to our Father is becoming more pronounced as his Spirit works in your life. And so you find yourself strengthened for what lies ahead, confident in his love that will endure forever.

> For the LORD is good
> and his love endures forever;
> his faithfulness continues through all generations.
> (Psalm 100:5)

The promise of God that he will complete the good work he has started in each of us means that we will always be discovering more about God's grace and love. And we will also always be discovering more about how to love God with our whole heart. We will find that even things we thought were great—like Trent's wife, Li, discovers in the next chapter—might be keeping us from the peace and satisfaction that is waiting for us as we grow in our trust and love for God.

CHAPTER 10

Satisfaction that Lasts More than a Moment

Trent's wife, Li, piped the last strand of hairy fur onto the Cookie Monster cake she was decorating for their three-year-old son's birthday party. Her hand was cramped from piping hundreds and hundreds of hair strands, blue icing was everywhere, and she was in a foul mood. The guests for Joseph's party would be there in thirty minutes and the kitchen was a mess, the younger kids weren't even bathed yet, and Li was covered with sticky frosting.

Li had started icing the cake that morning as soon as Lily and John left for school. This was the final day of prep for the party. Two months ago Li searched Pinterest and found ideas for the Cookie Monster party. Since then she obsessed in the myriad of details to pull off the perfect party. She fashioned gum paste figures to go with the cake, made Cookie Monster cake pops, sent out invitations accompanied by a homemade cookie, searched the Web for glass milk bottles and blue and white straws, created homemade party decorations and favors, and even had her nails done Cookie Monster blue with black eyes and mouth.

Li is a Pinterest addict. The site to "organize and share the things you love" has lured her to believe that the polished sheen of online images represents real life. Evidence of Li's obsession is plentiful. She repeatedly volunteers to bring the main dish to her small group Bible study dinners and then stays on Pinterest for hours to find new and impressive entrees, entrees that require so much time to prepare that she neglects doing the study. For the women's retreat Li insisted on sewing little zipper bags for all the attendees to hold the weekend's program and notebook. She made 250 zipper bags but was too exhausted to learn anything at the retreat or enjoy the fellowship. Instead, she vigilantly watched to see the women's reactions to the bags, unsatisfied if they didn't ooh and aah over them.

Today's efforts were typical of the time, energy, and attention to detail Li is consumed with in order to live the picture-perfect life. It was now 5:30. The day had not gone well. First, Li had problems with the consistency of the icing. It was too thin and all ran together, making her Cookie Monster cake look like a big blue blob. Even though she'd spent all morning on it, Li scraped all the icing off to start again.

However, Li didn't have enough powdered sugar to make a new batch of icing, so that meant loading Joseph and Evie into their car seats for a quick trip to the store. Before leaving the house, Li changed her clothes and carefully applied lipstick, annoyed at the time it took but unwilling to be seen in public with blue icing streaks on her jeans. Snapping at four-year-old Evie to hurry up, Li scooped up Joseph and belted him into his car seat. Evie tormented him all the way to the store and Li threatened and counted to three twice in the five-minute trip.

As if dealing with Evie wasn't enough, Joseph threw a temper tantrum in the middle of the baking aisle because he wanted colored marshmallows. Li was mortified by his behavior. Li knew he didn't even like colored marshmallows but to shut him up, she let him have his way.

By the time they got home from the store, it was noon and both kids were whining because they were hungry. Li was whining too, just not out loud. She quickly slapped something together for the kids' lunch and began a new batch of icing. When Evie complained that she didn't like peach jelly on her peanut butter sandwich, Li told her that if she heard one more word of complaint from her, she wouldn't get any birthday cake that night at Joseph's party.

Things hadn't gone any better during the afternoon. The new icing Li piped onto the cake started to peel away, leaving Cookie Monster

with big bald spots. After trying to patch it, Li wasn't satisfied with
how it looked and so she scraped everything off for the second time and
started over again.

Li thinks she can't be satisfied unless things are picture perfect. Li
lives in a constant state of discontent.

Li's problem is not that she wants to have a nice birthday party for
her son. Li's problem is not that choosing a Cookie Monster cake was
too difficult and she should have chosen something easier. Li's problem
goes so much deeper. She is not satisfied with God being in charge of
every circumstance in her life. She does not really believe that he has
given her *everything* she needs for life and godliness (2 Peter 1:3). She
is not satisfied with God's control of her life. She is not satisfied with
limits.

Satisfied with God's Rule and Power

Psalm 115:3 states: "Our God is in heaven; he does whatever pleases
him." Incomprehensibly, what pleases him is to love us and make us like
Christ.

Jerry Bridges makes the following noteworthy statement about
God's sovereignty, "God in His love always wills what is best for us. In
His wisdom He always knows what is best, and in His sovereignty He
has the power to bring it about."[14]

Yet Li has not been satisfied to be under God's control when his
control is contrary to her plans and desires. The Cookie Monster cake is
just one instance of Li's desire to do what pleases *her*. Today, Li planned
for Joseph's birthday party to include a perfect Cookie Monster cake,
and she was unwilling to have God redirect her plan.

After hours piping the icing onto the cake, Li had a disaster on her
hands when the icing ran together. Although Li was unaware of it, this
was a worship opportunity. This was an opportunity for Li to humbly
accept that God is in control of all things (including her blue blob of a
cake!) and to submit her plans and desires to him.

Proverbs 19:21 reports, "Many are the plans in a man's heart, but
it is the Lord's purpose that prevails." Li didn't stop to worship or

consider God's plans at the moment of disaster. Li was consumed with a cake that looked like a monster. (And, ironically, as the day went on, she became a "monster" in her actions and attitude toward her children.)

There were many points throughout the day where the Holy Spirit nudged Li's conscience, and she could have stopped her downward spiral into perfectionism by taking a moment to listen to the truth from God's Word he brought to mind. But as the icing ran together, Li functioned as if God could not be trusted to use his power for her good. She functionally ignored his authority over all of her life and clung to her plan for the icing so that she could have the picture-perfect party. Because she longed to be able to post pictures of her beautiful party on Pinterest, she resisted the Spirit's prompting to recognize that presenting the perfect cake for her company was less important than loving her children well.

Li's resistance to God's sovereignty and power seem foolish when we consider how God has chosen to use his power. God used his power to crush his beloved Son (Isaiah 53:10) so we could be rescued from sin and judgment and become his children and heirs (Romans 8:17). God has chosen to use his power to work all things, even blue blobs, for the good of those who love him (Romans 8:28).

Satisfied with Limits of Time and Ability

God has set Li in his creation within the limits of time—giving her twenty-four hours a day to enjoy and bring glory to him. Sometimes these limits are burdensome to Li and she fails to worship. She covets more time—more time to get things done just as she wants them done—the cake, the meal, the project, etc.—and she responds in ways that dishonor God when she doesn't have enough time to fulfill her desires. She may shirk her God-given responsibilities and priorities to spend extra time on the things that matter to her—the cake, the house, the project, etc.

We can all make all kinds of things more important than loving God and loving others. We can minimize our responsibilities to those closest to us—our spouse, our kids, our neighbors—in order to maximize the time spent on things that have smaller value in God's economy—the cake, the meal, the project. These can be powerful temptations. The day of Joseph's party, Li sacrificed parenting her children well to have the time to decorate Joseph's cake. She was not satisfied with the way God set up his universe. Of course the cake, the meal, the project, etc., could always be better if she devoted more time. But when Li takes from other God-given priorities and responsibilities to invest the time to "perfect" one special area, she has not worshipped God and submitted her life to his good plans. Instead she is worshipping herself and her control. This never ends well. It didn't end well for Li, and it doesn't end well for you and me either. Li ended her day frazzled by a cake and, as she thought about it, sad about the way she treated her children. How different her day would have gone if, as soon as she noticed that she was consumed with a perfect cake instead of loving and parenting her children, she had turned to her Father in heaven and asked for his Spirit to help her and change her.

Like Li, it's all too easy for us to distrust God's control of our lives. Our heavenly Father, the One who knows the beginning from the end, has distributed gifts and abilities as he has wisely determined is best. But we are often dissatisfied with God's distribution and instead covet what we believe are the best gifts.

We want it all. We want to become the Nobel Prize recipient in physics, a rock star, a Pulitzer Prize winner, the next Steve Jobs, and the coanchor of the ABC Nightly News. However, "God in His love always wills what is best for us. In His wisdom He always knows what is best, and in His sovereignty He has the power to bring it about."[15] Remembering this, reminding ourselves of this truth when we are tempted to want what God hasn't given us, helps us to be content where we are with the gifts and abilities God has entrusted to us.

We can humbly accept that there may be areas in our lives where we will never be superior. Not because we didn't try or work hard, but because God did not design each of us to excel in every way possible for a human. So we may never become a world-famous superstar. We may not even be the best cake decorator for our kids' birthdays. However, we can work diligently and joyfully within the limits of time and ability God has given and let God use our efforts as he sees fit.

Satisfied with Being Faithful

Because God has given the limits of time and ability, we have the opportunity to worship him by being faithful in all the areas of responsibility God entrusts to each of us. Li was tempted to neglect areas of responsibility in order to concentrate on making one area "perfect." Like Li, we can become absorbed in perfecting one area and neglect our responsibilities in other areas. We can spend all our time serving at church and never have a night at home with our families. Or, we can be so totally invested in the "perfect" family that we fail to serve anyone outside the home. We can get so busy shuffling the kids from one activity to another in order to give them a well-rounded upbringing, that we don't love our neighbors. It's not easy to sort this out, but all of us who are in Christ have his immediate help. We have his Spirit living in our hearts, giving us the power to be like Christ, to love like him and turn from our own agenda. Paul tells us that we need to keep in step with the Spirit and so not gratify our own desires (Galatians 5:25). We all need this help every day.

For Li keeping in step with the Spirit could start with looking at her schedule and considering how much time and energy she is giving to the various areas God has entrusted to her stewardship. Does the way she spends her time reflect God's priorities of loving him and loving others? How about you? What does your time and schedule say about your priorities? A great way to notice when you have gotten off track is to think about how much joy you have in serving. Keeping in step with the Spirit means we will see the fruit of the Spirit in our lives—love, joy, peace, patience, kindness, goodness, gentleness, faithfulness, and self-control. When you notice that the first two are missing—the love and the joy—you can be certain that you have gotten off track and aren't in step with the Spirit. Thankfully, although we turn from God to go our own way, he never turns from us. Let your irritation and lack of joy alert you to your need to turn to God, submit your time to him, ask him for forgiveness for getting off track, and ask for the Spirit so you can keep in step with his plans for your day.

As Li considers her schedule and thinks through how her day can reflect God's priorities, she will probably find it helpful to put limits on how much time she can devote to each responsibility that God has given her. Then Li can ask for the Spirit to guide her and help her so she can work faithfully and heartily to fill *all* her responsibilities, rather than one-sidedly seeking to "perfect" an area that is especially important to her. Of course, there will be times when emergencies require rearranging her schedule and temporarily emphasizing one responsibility over others, but this choice can also come from a heart that is depending on God for help and guidance.

Satisfied with God's Definition of Success, Not the World's Definition

Keeping in step with the Spirit may mean Li doesn't have the "perfect" birthday party for her son. It may mean serving blue blob cake so that she can love God and her children. It will probably mean that she won't conclude her day by posting pictures on Pinterest. For others, keeping in step with the Spirit may mean not getting the corner office at work. We may lose out on the corner office, not because we weren't diligent and faithful, but because keeping in step with the Spirit meant that we didn't devote *all* our time and energies to work; we also devoted ourselves to our family, our church, our neighbors, and our relationship with God.

Living with limits is a worship opportunity. By his divine power God has given us *everything* we need for life and godliness. Do we realize that "everything" is HIM?[16] As this realization grows deeper and deeper, we can be satisfied.

Part 3

CHAPTER 11

Paralyzed by Fear of Failure

I hate failure. Many of us believe that failure defines us as a loser. It's not that the project failed; it's that *I* failed. It's not that the decision was wrong; *I* am wrong. *I* am a failure. We loathe feeling like a failure. Failure is for people who are losers, for deadbeats, and underperformers. Who wants to be known as a loser? And we respond with fear.

Many of us are like Randy who lives with an internal voice telling him he is a failure. Randy's older brother is Trent, whom you may remember excelled in both academics and sports. His big brother was an A student and lettered in basketball and soccer. Randy wasn't gifted in academics or sports like his brother, but he lived with the expectation from others that he had the same talents as Trent. At the beginning of the school year, teachers who had had Trent as a pupil would often praise him to Randy and tell him they were looking forward to having him follow in his brother's footsteps. Gym teachers would single Randy out to demonstrate new skills, assuming Randy had the physical abilities of Trent. But Randy had neither Trent's academic gifts nor his athletic prowess. Some teachers were silently disappointed; others openly belittled him for not measuring up. One gym teacher, after singling him out as a leader, made him the object of his ridicule when it became obvious that he couldn't perform like his brother.

At home, Randy's parents frequently tried to motivate him by asking him why he couldn't be like his brother. Of course, their words only served to heighten Randy's performance anxiety.

Like Randy, fear of failure may be the companion who greets you with your morning coffee. You don't just hear the cashier asking if you want cream and sugar, you hear another voice predicting impending failure. Perhaps the voice started out as external—the father who could never be pleased, the big sister who was critical, the teacher who harshly rebuked, but it didn't take long for the voice to become internal. Even though the external voices may have stopped speaking long ago, the internal voice still haunts us.

How do you silence the voice inside your head? For most perfectionists, your knee-jerk response is to want to prove you're not a failure. It seems reasonable to you that the only way to mute the voice is to never fail, to be perfect. Surely if you don't ever fail the voice will quiet, perhaps even slink away chased by a new voice proclaiming you are capable and competent.

Opportunities present themselves to perform perfectly, to be successful and thus to silence the voice. But the opportunities make the voice grow louder. Now it becomes a bullhorn, "You'll probably mess up; you probably can't do it; you probably won't be successful." And fear grips your heart.

If you're like Randy, you may have learned to procrastinate to muffle the voice predicting failure. Randy has a project sitting on his desk right now that seems to sneer at him, "This is beyond your ability. The entire office will ridicule you when you can't figure this out." He would never have volunteered for the project, but he wasn't given a chance to say no. His boss had simply slid the project folder across the table in front of everyone at a departmental meeting saying, "Here, Randy, I'd like for you to take care of this."

Randy can feel the humiliation of his sixth-grade gym class returning to grip his heart. Randy can almost hear his sixth grade gym teacher saying, "Here, Randy, show the class how to climb the rope." Randy hadn't known how to climb the rope, nor had he had the upper body strength required. After three lame attempts, the gym teacher had pushed him aside and asked Kylee to demonstrate. She had shimmied to the top and back down while the rest of the class sniggered.

Now Randy tries to put tasks off until he can be confident of success. Action gets postponed until he feels he will perform perfectly. "Don't try until you know you won't fail!" has become Randy's mantra. But deadlines approach before he's confident of success, and Randy is often left scrambling, hurriedly trying to pull something together.

In many ways, failure due to procrastination is less personal for Randy. Failing because he did a hasty, last-minute job after procrastinating is less unsettling than working his hardest and flat-out failing. Failures due to procrastination leave the door open to thinking, "I could have been a success if I had longer." But failure after working diligently can't be dismissed or minimized. If I try my best and still fail, I can't tell myself that it's because I didn't have enough time. I'm just a failure. That's the bottom line.

Sadly the voice is right—we are all losers who don't measure up. Created to reflect God's glory, to be his image, we have all failed to live up to our most basic commission. We have failed to reflect the glory of God. We have all fallen short in our purpose. We don't love God with all our heart, mind, soul, and strength and we don't love others like we love ourselves. We are failures. How pitiful to assume that any lesser success could ever silence the voice. No wonder fear of failure paralyzes us. No wonder we try to play it safe.

However, for those who have turned to God and cried out for his salvation and received it through faith in Christ as a free gift, failure is no longer our identity. We have a Savior who has taken our failure, shame, embarrassment, and disgrace upon himself. We now have the identity of Christ. We have been dressed in his success, his righteousness, his perfection (Isaiah 61:10). Not our success—his! Now our call is to believe by faith that everything that belongs to Christ is ours as well. To continue to call ourselves failures when we have been clothed with Christ is to turn away from all we have been given. It just doesn't make sense!

Playing it safe is often a sign of unbelief. As those who follow Christ, our lives should be on a trajectory of increasing trust and dependence on God, as we move forward in faith-filled obedience. Often, if you refuse to try, you refuse to trust. If your life is characterized by a "play it safe" mentality, this may be a good time to reevaluate whether or not you have truly put your trust in Christ. Take some time to consider what is really holding you back from trusting him. Stepping out in trust may seem dangerous, but is life really so much better lived in "safety"?

The Bible is full of people who tried and failed—often spectacularly—as they learned to follow God. Many of them experienced times where they refused to move forward out of fear. But as they pushed through their fear and discomfort into obedience by God's work in their hearts, through faith they came to know God more intimately and desire him more. It is through this process that we gain a fuller knowledge of and connection to God and to each other, and it is through these relatively small steps of faith that the bigger story of God's redeeming love unfolds. It may seem safer not to engage, not to try, but the greater danger lies in continually refusing to trust God.

Instead of being controlled by our fears, we can ask our Father for his help, for the Spirit to be at work in us so we can step forward in courage and faithfulness. So we can take the scary first step of starting a project we don't really know how to do or attempting to learn a new skill. And if we fail (and of course we will, we are human), then we have a Savior who forgives and helps.

We Do Not Know What to Do!

You might be thinking about what you are facing right now and wondering exactly how you will find the courage to move forward or even to know what to do next. The Bible record of Judah's good king Jehoshaphat gives us a great model for how to move forward when we don't know what to do with circumstances that threaten to overwhelm.

In 2 Chronicles 20 we find that the country of Judah is about to be attacked. Judah's king, Jehoshaphat learns that a coalition of nations is advancing against him and a large army is getting ready to attack him. As king, he knows what happens when an army overtakes you—there is slaughter, rape, the bellies of pregnant women are ripped open, men are commanded to lie down so that the victors can parade across their backs crushing their internal organs, women and children are taken captive into slavery, dead bodies are left like refuse in the streets, kings are tortured and killed. If there was ever a time to fear failure, this would have been appropriate. Being a loser in this situation will have grave consequences.

Jehoshaphat has to come up with a battle plan but he doesn't know what to do (2 Chronicles 20:12). We've been there too, haven't we? While we may not face a vast army of allied enemies, we're regularly faced with tasks we don't know how to accomplish. We don't know what to do either. Perhaps we can take lessons from Jehoshaphat who didn't know what to do, lessons from a man who didn't want to fail.

First, Jehoshaphat had to overcome the paralysis that comes with the fear of failure. With the cold grip of terror squeezing his heart, Jehoshaphat had to determine what he would do first. What was Jehoshaphat's first step? What would you do if you were on the brink of battle against a vast army that seemed impossible to defeat? What do you typically do when you don't know how to perform perfectly?

Here's what Jehoshaphat did. He turned to God (2 Chronicles 20:3). Various versions use different words for what Jehoshaphat did—set his face (ESV), turned his attention (NASB), set himself to seek (NKJV), resolved (NIV)—but all indicate that Jehoshaphat made a calculated mental decision. This was his first step. He determined to turn to God. The fact that Jehoshaphat had to resolve to turn to God shows that turning to God may not be a natural response. Often when we are struggling, we forget we have a heavenly Father who is more powerful than any army and more for us than our closest friend. Paralysis and fear begin to break when we remember that we have an all-powerful Father in heaven who cares for us and hears our cries for help.

Jehoshaphat was not going to God with a battle plan and asking God to bless it. He didn't know what to do. Jehoshaphat simply resolved to turn to God. You could do that too. You could turn your attention to God.

Next we see Jehoshaphat crying out to God. He begins his cry by going to God in prayer and affirming that God is the ruler of everything. Jehoshaphat affirmed that power and might are in God's hand, not the hands of the vast armies coming even now to attack him. You too can remember and even say out loud that God is the ruler of everything and that all power and might are in his hand. When you do this, you are entering his courts with praise.

Then, Jehoshaphat described his situation to God. (An alliance of nations is marching on Judah.) You too can describe your situation to God. You can tell him what task, problem, or circumstance you've been given and describe what is frightening to you. Jehoshaphat reminded God that these armies were marching against people whom God loved. As God's treasured possession, you too can remind God that you are his beloved.

Then Jehoshaphat acknowledges that he is powerless. He is powerless to overcome such a huge army. He is powerless to save his country from defeat. You can do that too. Remind God that you are a frail, weak creature, totally dependent on his love, mercy, and grace. After that, Jehoshaphat explains he is clueless. He doesn't know what to do. You can certainly do that. Finally, Jehoshaphat concludes by telling God that his trust is in him. You can do that too!

Jehoshaphat cries, "We do not know what to do, but our eyes are on you" (2 Chronicles 20:12). We too can cry, "We do not know what to do, but our eyes are on you."

What happened when Jehoshaphat cried out? What was the outcome? God declared the battle was the Lord's. God said, "Do not be afraid; do not be discouraged. Go out to face them tomorrow, and the LORD will be with you" (2 Chronicles 20:17).

The point here is not that God is going to slay armies before you. The point is that God answered Jehoshaphat when he cried out. In those days, before the completion of the Bible, God's answers and encouragement came through prophets. Now that we have the completed Word of God, we receive God's encouragement and answers through it. God wants us to learn from the examples and instruction he has provided in his Word. He is an unchangeable God. We don't have to be concerned that the process Jehoshaphat used will go out of date. God doesn't change, so cry out.

- Resolve to turn to God.
- Pray, remember, and say that God owns everything and that he is in control.
- Describe your situation.
- Remind God that you are his beloved because you have trusted in Christ and are therefore beloved by him.
- Acknowledge you are powerless.
- Tell God you don't know what to do.
- Tell God you trust in him.

Jehoshaphat's spirit of fear changed as he turned to God. God's grace came to him in power and love. Paul says the same thing in his letter to Timothy many centuries later. Paul reminds us that those who belong to God do not have a spirit of fear but of power, love, and self-control (2 Timothy 1:7). These three gifts of God's grace—power, love, and self-control—are promises to us. These are the most amazing gifts that anyone could receive—they are part of what we receive when we turn to Christ in faith. They are so amazing that they need a whole chapter all to themselves.

CHAPTER 12

A Spirit of Power, Love, and Self-control Instead of the Paralysis of Fear

A Spirit of Power

Randy grew up feeling powerless. He knew he didn't have his brother Trent's skills and abilities, yet he was expected to perform as if he did. Everyone around him seemed to assume his lack of performance was his fault. They didn't really understand Randy's strengths and weaknesses.

We have a Savior who knows us intimately. He knows what we can handle and what we can't handle. He knows how far we can be pushed before we break. And he promises that he won't put more on us than we can handle with his help (1 Corinthians 10:13).

Our faithful God won't break his promise. He won't renege. He won't go back on his word. He backs up his promise with his power. The full faith and credit of his greatness stands behind this promise.

God excels in power (Romans 1:20). He's so good at power that sometimes those closest to him just refer to him as Power (Mark 14:62 ESV). Because he excels in power he can make statements like "nothing is impossible with God" with an assurance that's not trash talk. All power belongs to him.

It is often the very things that trigger the greatest fear of failure that give you an opportunity to see God excel in power. Jehoshaphat experienced this. He was no match for the vast armies coming against him, but God's power was brightly displayed in what happened. Paul tried to communicate this when he said, "For when I am weak, then I am strong" (2 Corinthians 12:10).

Don't you often feel your weakest when your fear of failure is strongest? You need God's grace when your fear of failure grows strong. In fact, his grace, his help, is all you need—it is sufficient (2 Corinthians 12:9). The great power of God transcends your ineptitude. Your lack of ability or perfection is not fatal, it is not a fault, a flaw, or a hindrance; it is essential. God's power is made *perfect* in weakness (2 Corinthians 12:9–10). God designed us as jars of clay, fragile and easily broken, to show that this surpassing power is from him, not from us (2 Corinthians 4:7).

To use God's power properly, we need to address two roadblocks that will prevent us from witnessing his power. First, God makes his power available to us for the display of his glory and splendor (Isaiah 63), not to make us look good. In Randy's heart, he can still hear the echo of his sniggering classmates. He never wants to live through that again. He never again wants to look like an idiot in front of others—not anywhere, not anyplace, not any time. So Randy has tried to build walls to protect himself. He doesn't want to take risks or make himself vulnerable. But Randy's walls are a roadblock that prevents God's power from being displayed through his life. When Randy hides behind walls, no one can see God's great splendor. However, when Randy turns and cries out to God for help not to hide, God's power will begin to become evident.

The second roadblock that will prevent us from witnessing God's power is that sometimes our standard of evaluation misleads us and causes us to draw the wrong conclusion. There are a variety of standards available to evaluate success and failure. Perhaps some of the standards on the following list are ones you have used.

- my perception
- my experience
- my wisdom
- others' perceptions
- others' experience
- others' wisdom
- good outcomes
- bad outcomes
- others are pleased
- others are not pleased
- I feel good
- I feel bad
- it worked
- it didn't work
- things went smoothly
- things didn't go smoothly
- others think well of me
- others don't think well of me
- the *right* people think well of me
- the *right* people don't think well of me . . .

The list goes on. Using data from all these sources may be helpful or may be misleading.

According to 1 Corinthians 1:19, human perceptions and human wisdom aren't trustworthy. In fact, God calls our wisdom foolish (1 Corinthians 1:20). We can easily be deceived. So data from ourselves and others may or may not be trustworthy. To complicate matters, things sometimes look like failures when they are not. (Remember Christ's death on the cross?) So how do we figure out what is failure and what is not?

We must train ourselves to make judgments based on the Word of truth—on the Word given to us by the Father who doesn't change. If we use his Word as our standard of failure or success, we can be confident our evaluations are accurate.

According to his Word, the bottom line is this: we are only successful when we do what we were created to do—glorify him. We are only failures when we fail to do what God created us to do—glorify him. That's it. We're not successful if we're rich (Luke 12 describes the rich man with overflowing barns as a fool), we're not successful if we're beautiful (Proverbs 31 says beauty is worthless), we're not successful if we're polished and poised (Proverbs 31 says charm is deceitful), we're not successful if others approve of us (Proverbs 27:6 explains that enemies flatter, making it look like they approve of us) or for any other reason. We are only truly successful when we reflect God's image.

In the end, we are not failures if our projects don't work; we are not failures if our kids don't make the team; we are not failures if our shoes aren't polished or our lawn has weeds. We are failures if we fail to glorify God. Randy will not be a failure if his project fails. Randy will be a failure if he focuses on himself—on what will happen to him, on what others will think of him—instead of focusing on loving God and loving others. If he focuses on loving God by expressing his confidence and trust in God's power to help him and loving others by working to the best of his abilities with the skills he currently has to accomplish his boss's project, Randy will never be a failure according to God and his Word.

As we begin to let go of all other definitions of success and use God's standard, our confidence can grow. We no longer need to be paralyzed by the thought of what others may think. We will be confident that even in disgraceful suffering we have the opportunity to experience the grace of the gospel. We will recall how Jesus suffered for us, leaving us an example so that we can follow in his footsteps. We will entrust ourselves to him who judges justly.

A Spirit of Love

In the past, Randy's fear of failure has suffocated his love for God and others because his fear has diverted his attention to his reputation, his name, his honor. Randy has been paralyzed by what others might think of him. I, too, often fear failure because of what might happen to me. Fear asks, What will I lose? How will I be hurt? What if I fail? What's going to happen to me?

Listen to how our powerful Father answers these questions. Because of God's love and grace, here's what is going to happen to all who belong to God, to all who belong to Christ.

- We are going to reign with God as a coheir with Christ (Romans 8:17).

- We are going to be seated in the heavenly realms (Ephesians 2:4–7) and enjoy pleasures at God's right hand forevermore (Psalm 16).

- We are going to have God walking with us through deep waters and commanding them not to sweep us away (Isaiah 43).

- We are going to see the incomparable riches of God's grace (Ephesians 2).

- We are going to be loved with an everlasting love (Romans 8).

- We are going to a place prepared for us by Christ (John 14).

These promises put us in a place where we can allow God to quiet our fears with his love.

> The LORD your God is with you,
>   he is mighty to save.
> He will take great delight in you,
>   he will quiet you with his love,
>   he will rejoice over you with singing.
> (Zephaniah 3:17)

As a result we can confidently say, "The Lord is my helper; I will not be afraid; what can man do to me?" (Hebrews 13:6).

Fear can squelch love, but love can smother fear. So allow love to turn your focus outward. Begin asking new questions. How can I give? How can I help? What can I do for others? What do I need to do right now to move this project forward in order to serve others? As you ask these questions and follow through in love, you will find that fear's power is being broken.

A Spirit of Self-Control

Moving forward in love may be difficult and frightening. In his goodness, God has also gifted us with another powerful tool we'll need in order to not be overcome by fear of failure. God has given us the gift of self-control.

It will take self-control to set your face toward God and cry out to him. Like Randy, your natural response is likely to be panic. You panic because you're facing an assignment you don't know how to complete and it seems overwhelming. You might be exposed as imperfect. But God has not put a curse on you; he has not given you a spirit of fear. God has treated you with goodness. He has given you a spirit of power and of love and of self-control. Therefore, you can face God and cry out to him.

Even though Randy has a long history of being judged as a failure by others, God can help him begin to exercise self-control. After all, self-control is one of the fruits of the Spirit that is God's gift to us as we turn to him. Randy can ask God for the self-control to believe that God won't give him more than he can handle and will always provide the resources necessary for any struggle. Then Randy can choose to believe the words of his faithful Father—he will not let Randy be tempted beyond his ability to withstand (1 Corinthians 10:13).

When you are tempted to believe another voice besides God, you can ask your Father in heaven for the self-control to trust that he will never let the righteous fall and even to believe that God is talking about you when he is talking about the righteous. In Christ you are righteous. As Paul says, it's not a righteousness of your own that comes from the law, but that which comes through faith in Christ, the righteousness from God that depends on faith (Philippians 3:9). Because of this righteousness that comes through faith in Christ, God is talking about you when he talks about the righteous. He will never permit the righteous to fall (Psalm 55:22).

It will take the spirit of self-control that God gives you to admit your weakness, to admit you don't know what to do. As the Spirit of God works in you, you can control how you think. You can see your weakness not as a flaw, but as essential for the display of God's power and trust that God's power is truly made perfect in weakness. You can believe God's grace is sufficient (2 Corinthians 12:9–10), that it is enough, it is all that is needed. You can move ahead confidently. You don't need something else. God's help is not inferior or insufficient. God's grace is adequate. He is not inept. He is not lacking in knowledge. He is not weak or ineffective.

We need self-control to evaluate success and failure using God's standard rather than another standard. It takes self-control to take risks and possibly see things not turn out the way we wanted—the way that makes us look good. It takes self-control to recognize that apparent failure in terms of human evaluation is only genuinely failure if we don't glorify God. It takes self-control to long for God's glory, not our own glory. It takes self-control to delight ourselves in the Lord (Psalm 37:4). But when we do these things—when we purpose to think like God does about ourselves and his world, then we get the best—a life that brings glory to God, no matter what others might think and say.

Where do you need self-control right now? Is it to get started on a project when you are not sure how to do the entire thing? It will take self-control for you to do the next right thing, rather than putting tasks off until you feel more confident and are sure you won't fail. It will take self-control to go and humbly ask questions when you get stuck and aren't sure what the next step should be. It will take self-control to persevere and not quit.

How do you get a new spirit of power, love, and self-control? You probably already know that these things don't come naturally to you. But the good news is that when you come to Christ in faith, when you turn from your sins, and ask him to live in your heart, you get a new Spirit—the Spirit of Christ. That's where you get the power, love, and self-control that aren't natural to you. The Holy Spirit is the Father's marvelous gift and he is ours for the asking (Luke 11:13). And, according to Jesus, we need to keep on asking (Luke 11:9–10). This is a daily struggle—to turn away from our fears and turn toward Jesus and ask for his Spirit to change and help—but as you do so, you will get to experience the truth of 1 Corinthians 10:13: God is faithful and he won't give us more than we can handle. Not giving us more than we can handle doesn't mean God won't give us hard things to do. However, when God does give us hard things, he will help us. And we can be certain God will help us because he is faithful.

The end result is blessing. Rather than fearing failure we will have feared the Lord and delighted in him. According to Psalm 112:1, we are blessed. We have the privilege of seeing God's exceeding power at work in us! So use your weaknesses to show God's power (2 Corinthians 12:9). He is able to do far more than you can imagine (Ephesians 3:20).

CHAPTER 13

Bryce and Angela: Two Ways of Trying to Look Good to Others

Bryce surreptitiously surveyed the restaurant to see if others were look-ing their direction. He and Angela were having a reunion dinner with three of his old college roommates and their wives. The evening hadn't started very well. Angela had asked Bryce if her new outfit made her look fat. Since Bryce didn't like the outfit, he told her yes. Big mistake. That set Angela off. She accused him of not really caring about her. Ac-cording to Angela, the only person he cared about was himself.

Bryce felt like he didn't really need this right now. He'd had a hard day at work full of backroom negotiations trying to get his colleagues to buy into his way of handling a client. Then he had to spend way too much time pointing out errors in a report his personal assistant had typed. Bryce was mad. It shouldn't have to be his job to teach her how to make a report look good. As if that weren't enough, some bozo caused an accident on the interstate, making Bryce late getting home.

Bryce didn't want Angela to blow this evening with his college roommates. Bryce remembered the good-natured jests from his bud-dies when he and Angela got engaged. "I see you've gone out and gotten yourself a trophy wife." "How'd an ugly cuss like you get such a good-looking woman?" Bryce had enjoyed their ribbing and he didn't want to lose their envy by showing up with Angela in an outfit he thought made her look dumpy.

Bryce believes he "needs" others to think he is successful—an up-and-coming employee, a good husband, a model Christian. The only way Bryce knows to pull this off is to try to control everyone around him so they don't make him look bad. His colleagues need to follow his lead, his wife needs to look good, and his personal assistant better not make any typos.

As he surveyed the restaurant, Bryce was glad he had gotten Angela to wear something different. He caught a few of the envious glances of other men and knew they wished Angela belonged to them. With Angela in her black dress, Bryce was proud to have her on his arm.

Bryce wants Angela and everyone else to do for him what he was created to do for God—to give him honor, and to worship him. Created to glorify God, our sin-broken hearts now desire to get glory for ourselves, not to reflect God's glory. Like Bryce, this kind of thinking comes so naturally to me that often I don't even realize how consumed I am with how I appear to others and what they are thinking about me. Without even noticing, I have put my glory in the place of reflecting God's glory. I have become a glory thief. How about you? Have you noticed how easily this can happen in your life as well?

Some of us are like Bryce, demanding that everyone around us makes us look good. Spouse, children, employees—all must make us look good. There is no room to mess up and no grace for mistakes because proud people believe their personal glory is tarnished if someone close to them messes up. You better not make them look bad. They demand perfection from themselves and everyone around them.

This proud attitude seems to be strikingly absent in other perfectionists. Angela is like this. She loves to cook, but is never satisfied with how things turn out. When she prepares a wonderful meal, she will never accept a compliment. Instead she talks about how the potatoes were too brown. Perhaps you have noticed this in yourself and others. Some people, when asked to take on new responsibility, point out their weaknesses rather than jumping at the chance to assume an important role. Even when they perform well, rather than enjoying the admiration of others, they are quick to point out the weak spots in their performance. The musician who performed a difficult sonata frets that she missed a note. The executive who has landed millions in sales broods over the lost prospect, and the parent of a student headed to an Ivy League college regrets his child was salutatorian rather than valedictorian. Clearly, these perfectionists are not boasting about how great they are. Yet they may not be much different than Bryce when the desires of their hearts are revealed. Although this might appear to be true humility, this is actually pride masquerading as humility.

False Humility

This is an easy trap to fall into. Even Moses, who the Bible describes in Numbers 12:3 as the most humble man on earth, wasn't humble on every occasion in every situation. As you may know, God personally called Moses to bring his people out of Egypt, to free them from slavery. When God called him, Moses had been living in another country for forty years because he had fled from Egypt after killing an Egyptian who was beating one of his own Hebrew people.

Appearing to Moses in a burning bush, God commissioned Moses saying, "And now the cry of the Israelites has reached me, and I have seen the way the Egyptians are oppressing them. So now, go. I am sending you to Pharaoh to bring my people the Israelites out of Egypt" (Exodus 3:9–10).

Not surprisingly, Moses had a number of questions about his assignment and God answered his questions, giving him lots of assurance and drawing Moses's attention back to himself—the Powerful One who would actually be the Deliverer of the people through Moses. After hearing God's assurances and being given the ability to do miraculous signs in order to convince the Israelites he had been sent by God, Moses still had this objection "O Lord, I have never been eloquent, neither in the past nor since you have spoken to your servant. I am slow of speech and tongue" (Exodus 4:10).

Although we can't say for sure, this appears to be false humility on Moses's part. It had the appearance of humility because Moses pointed out his weaknesses, not his strengths. Moses told God he was slow of speech. I suspect that it is false humility because the focus doesn't seem to be God's glory. (A statement that could glorify God might go something like this, "Lord, you know I've never been too articulate, therefore it seems to me I can't do what you're asking. But I know that you can do all things and if you want to use someone like me who is not eloquent, I'm willing to obey.")

God answers Moses's objection by drawing Moses's attention back to himself once again. "The LORD said to him, 'Who gave man his mouth? Who makes him deaf or mute? Who gives him sight or makes him blind? Is it not I, the LORD? Now go; I will help you speak and will teach you what to say" (Exodus 4:11–12).

Rather than being encouraged by this and believing and trusting in the Lord, Moses responded, "O Lord, please send someone else to do it" (Exodus 4:13). Asking God to send someone else to do such an important job seems like it could be an expression of humility. Clearly Moses wasn't trying to grab any glory for himself. Isn't that humble? But this time we know for sure that this was not a humble statement because it made God angry. Verse 14 tells us the Lord's anger burned against Moses when he made this statement. It is not humble to ask for someone else to do the job when God promises to help you speak and to teach you what to say (as he did in verses 11–12). It is unbelief and distrust.

Since God doesn't speak to us today by appearing in a burning bush and giving us direction, what would false humility look like in the twenty-first century? Today God speaks through his Word, so like Moses we would be displaying false humility whenever we say we can't do something God directs us to do in his Word. We exhibit false humility when we point out a weakness in ourselves when we ought to be directing people to the strength and glory of God.

While we want to be sure we don't get out of balance by neglecting to identify where and how changes need to be made to glorify God, some folks steal glory from God by never praising God for what he enables them to do.

The Heart of the Issue

The crux of the matter here is what is going on inside of us. Although others can't always discern our motives (1 Corinthians 2:11), God can and does (1 Chronicles 28:9). Not only does he understand our motives, he evaluates us by them (Jeremiah 17:10). For many perfectionists (and nonperfectionists) a desire for personal glory, a desire to look good and be held in high esteem resides in the secret recesses of our hearts. So we are happy when we look good (like Bryce with Angela). We are afraid if we think we might not look good (which leads us to point out our weaknesses when asked to assume more responsibility). And we are shamed if we look bad (we fret about potatoes that were too brown). We're always concerned about how we look. We care about our glory.

The sad truth is that in one way or another we're all glory thieves. All of us are prone to think of ourselves more highly than we ought and reflect God's glory less than we ought. However, we rarely see this in ourselves. We think we are humble if we don't boast or if we draw attention to our weaknesses. But if we could look into our hearts honestly, we'd probably find that we're a whole lot more like Bryce than we'd care to admit. Like Bryce, we want people to hold us in high esteem. Like Bryce, we don't want our glory messed up in any way. Naturally we want those around us to make us look good. Yet, when we pursue our glory we tarnish God's glory. God is not honored when we look good to others but our motives and desires are focused on our own glory.

Coming face-to-face with our desire for our own glory can be difficult. A love for our own honor is often concealed so adroitly that it's almost impossible to uncover. We also find that this desire is adept at concealing itself in new ways, which leads us to believe it's gone. Through his Holy Spirit, God offers to show us our sin and clothe us with *his* humility and honor. The one person who never stole glory from God in his life is Jesus. He was always perfectly humble. Christ serves as our example of how to clothe ourselves in his wardrobe. Coregent with God the Father, he did not consider his position something he graspingly had to hang onto. He was willing to let it go. He exchanged the nature of a King for the nature of a servant. The Creator of life humbled himself and willingly died so we could be released from the need to have others think we're successful.

Philippians 2:5–11 beautifully describes this:

> Your attitude should be the same as that of Christ Jesus:
> Who, being in very nature God,
> did not consider equality with God something to be grasped,
> but made himself nothing,
> taking the very nature of a servant,
> being made in human likeness.
> And being found in appearance as a man,
> he humbled himself
> and became obedient to death—
> even death on a cross!
> Therefore God exalted him to the highest place
> and gave him the name that is above every name,
> that at the name of Jesus every knee should bow,
> in heaven and on earth and under the earth,
> and every tongue confess that Jesus Christ is Lord,
> to the glory of God the Father.

Through God's grace you can grow in the same perfectly humble attitude displayed by Jesus Christ. With God's help, instead of working to guard your personal glory, you can increasingly live for the glory of the King of the universe. This is what it means to be humble; this is what it looks like to wear the King's robe. Truly humble people are not focused on how they look to others; they are concerned about how God looks to others. They want their lives to shine so that others see their good works and glorify the Father (Matthew 5:16). Through God's grace this can become more and more true of you.

Growing in True Humility

What might this look like for Angela? Whether the potatoes were too brown or not, Angela can still respond with how grateful she is that God has blessed her with a love of cooking. Or, Angela could direct attention to God by saying how thankful she is that God provides so

many flavors, textures, and tastes for us to enjoy. This won't come naturally to Angela; our natural response to all of life is to be self-focused.
But because Angela is a daughter of the King, she can grow in letting
her light shine before others so they will see her good works and praise
her Father. God directs us to reflect his image. God directs us that when
others see our good works they should praise our Father in heaven. It
is false humility to use God's grace and strength to do good works and
then focus solely on the wrong things you did or, worse yet, claim that
the right things God enabled you to do weren't good.

God told Moses to go and lead his people out of Egypt, and Moses
focused on his weakness. So, when we hear ourselves focusing on our
weaknesses a warning bell ought to go off that we may be in danger of
false humility. Remember that when Moses focused on his weaknesses,
the next statement out of his mouth made God angry. Moses asked God
to let someone else do what God wanted done. Moses's heart was full
of unbelief and distrust.

Today, God has asked us to love him and to love others (Matthew
22:37–39). Do we say things like, "I'm no good at reaching out to new
people [focus on my weakness], let someone else sit next to the new
person in church [let someone else do what God wants]." "I don't handle
conflict well [focus on my weakness], let someone else work with that
difficult person at work [let someone else do what God wants]." "I'm
not good at praying out loud [focus on my weakness], let someone else
pray before we eat [let someone else do what God wants]."

Of course, these examples are all simply applications of loving others, but if we hear ourselves regularly focusing on our weaknesses, we
may want to question whether we're displaying false humility, unbelief,
and distrust.

False humility comes from a heart consumed with how I look to
other people. False humility occurs when I use my weaknesses as a reason for not doing something I don't want to do or am afraid to do.

False humility can also be used to try to erect a wall of protection in
case we fail. If, when we're asked to do something, we point out how
unqualified we are, we may simply be trying to save ourselves from

humiliation if we fail. Thus, if we don't achieve what is expected, we can always say, "I told you I couldn't do this," and then it becomes the other person's fault for insisting we take on a job for which we were clearly unqualified. We save face.

The point here is not that the statements or words are necessarily wrong. What's important is the desires and motives that led to the statements. When we hear someone make deprecating comments about themselves, we won't necessarily be able to tell the underlying motives so it would be wrong to judge them. However, we should probably stop and examine ourselves if we have a tendency to make self-deprecating statements.

We might want to ask:

- How does this self-deprecating statement glorify God and lead others to think highly of him?
- How does this self-deprecating statement build others up by focusing on their needs and interests?
- Is there any possibility that I made this self-deprecating statement because I was primarily concerned with what other people think of me?
- Is there any possibility that I made this self-deprecating statement from a heart of fear rather than a spirit of power, love, and self-control?
- How does this statement show love for God and others?

False humility tries to cover up a focus on oneself by pointing out personal weaknesses but its underlying motive is not a concern for God's glory but a concern for self.

Moses would have other times in his leadership of the Israelites in which he was not humble (see Numbers 20 for example). Nevertheless, God did describe Moses as the most humble man on earth. So let's look for ways this was true in Moses's life and see what we can learn from his example that would help us grow in this humility that reflects the same attitude of Jesus. Of course, like Moses, we will not always be perfectly humble, but like Moses, we can still be used by God in significant ways.

CHAPTER 14

Lessons from a Humble Man

Once Bryce and Angela got to dinner and Bryce felt confident Angela looked good, he began to relax. He'd had a hard day up to this point, but he anticipated that his day would finally become enjoyable. Unfortunately, that didn't last long. His college buddies soon began telling stories that Bryce would rather be forgotten forever. They laughed as they recalled one embarrassing event after another while Bryce's sense of disgrace grew stronger and stronger. Although outwardly he laughed with everyone else, Bryce was mortified. He wished the evening had never happened. No form of disgrace was acceptable to him, even if it came in the form of good-natured jests. If we are honest with ourselves, most of us are more like Bryce than Moses. We don't want to be even mildly disgraced. But Moses was willing to accept disgrace if that meant that God was honored.

The Most Humble Man on Earth

To grow in this heart attitude, let's see what we can learn from the man God said was the most humble man on the face of the earth. This man, Moses, began life as a son of slaves. He was born in Egypt to Hebrew parents at a time when the Hebrews were slaves to the Egyptians. Being a slave during that time meant hard physical labor, overseen by ruthless masters who were brutal, merciless, cruel, and unfeeling.

Pharaoh, Egypt's ruler, was a prime example of the brutality of these masters. He mercilessly issued an order to throw every boy born to a slave woman into the river to drown. Pregnant at the time the order was issued, Moses's mother didn't know whether giving birth would mean rejoicing or anguish, celebration or panic. With no ultrasound to tell them their baby's sex in advance, these parents wouldn't know until delivery whether they could expect their baby to live or be seized and killed. The day came. Moses's mother went into labor. Her water broke. She delivered what the Bible describes as an exceptional baby—an exceptional baby boy. Determined to preserve the life of her baby, Moses's mom hid Moses in a basket in the river.

Moses's river bassinet was discovered by Pharaoh's daughter, who decided to take him home and raise him as her own child. What a contrast for Moses, from death row to king's grandson; from slave to prince. Raised as a grandson to the king, Moses grew up to be "more humble than anyone on the face of the earth." Are you startled by that statement? How many world leaders or their children do you know who are more humble than anyone on the face of the earth? For God to make such a statement about Moses is remarkable. What was it about Moses that made him so humble?

Willing to Accept Disgrace

The amazing thing about Moses is that he didn't cling to his royal position. We learn in Hebrews that Moses chose to be identified with God's people instead of being known as Pharaoh's son:

> By faith Moses, when he had grown up, refused to be known as the son of Pharaoh's daughter. He chose to be mistreated along with the people of God rather than to enjoy the pleasures of sin for a short time. He regarded disgrace for the sake of Christ as of greater value than the treasures of Egypt, because he was looking ahead to his reward. (Hebrews 11:24–26)

The Hebrews were the lowlifes in Egypt, and Moses chose to identify himself with them rather than enjoy his royal status. How many
high-level managers do you know who hang out with the company jani-
tors? How many CEOs regularly lunch with the employees in the secre-
tarial pool? Moses chose to identify himself with slaves, rather than with
royalty. He didn't forget where he came from.

What about us, do we forget where we came from? Do we forget
that we came to God without hope except in Jesus's death for us? Do we
do our best to give the impression that we've got our act together? Do
we want everyone around us to think highly of us? Do we shudder at the
thought of publicly messing up? I know this is often true of me. In those
times, I've forgotten where I came from.

To remember where we came from we must be willing to admit
that we are former slaves who have been adopted by God. Our slavery wasn't to a cruel Egyptian master. According to Romans 7:14, we
were all slaves to sin. We have "needed" people to think we're successful.
We've "needed" people to give us approval. We've "needed" people to
give us significance. And those "needs" have ruled us. Anything about us
that now looks like royalty is what has been given to us by our heavenly
Father.

Moses chose to be identified and mistreated with the Hebrew people, but this doesn't mean we should see Moses as some misguided mas-
ochist. It means we should take a hard look at what we treasure. When
God describes Moses in the book of Hebrews, he says Moses regarded
disgrace for the sake of Christ as of greater value than the treasures of
Egypt. In Moses's mind, being disgraced for Christ had more value than
wealth and prestige.

What do you treasure? Like me, do you struggle with treasuring the
high regard of others more than your identity in Christ? Go to God and
ask him to show you where you are going wrong. God will show you
your sin and he will give you the gift of repenting (turning from it) if
you ask. He will help you learn to assign value accurately. As you grow
in treasuring Christ, you can learn the grace of being humble even when
criticized.

Humble When Criticized

As we've seen, God appointed Moses to free the Hebrew people from slavery. Not only that, Moses was to lead them to God's Promised Land, a good and spacious land where the people could be rich and prosperous. So Moses (along with his brother Aaron) became the leader of the Hebrews. There were about two million or so Hebrews by then, slaves to the Egyptians. Moses acted as God's ambassador to Pharaoh (a different king than when he grew up), and after ten plagues and a death threat from Pharaoh that he would kill him on sight, Moses led the Israelites (or Hebrews) out of Egypt to freedom.

In his role as leader, Moses was frequently criticized. It seems like every time he turned around the Israelites were mad at him about something—sometimes it was about food, sometimes it was about water, sometimes it was about enemies. The Israelites were quick to believe the worst, and they regularly abused Moses verbally. On more than one occasion they wanted to fire him as their leader, and in some instances, they wanted to kill him.

Suppose everyone in your company decided it was your fault the company wasn't making money. Although you have been working hard and fulfilling the requirements of your job with excellence, when the economy turns sour, you get blamed because the company didn't make a profit in the third quarter. For some reason you don't understand, every employee in the company blames you because sales are down. Suppose you get called into a company meeting and royally chewed out. How would you respond?

For most of us, unfair criticism is a powerful temptation to counter with a proud, defensive response. We feel driven to make ourselves look better. Moses's response to criticism on those occasions demonstrates humility. Time and time again, when Moses was verbally abused, he didn't take it personally, he responded without defensiveness, and glorified God.

Exodus 16 gives an example of this. In this chapter the Israelites were traveling across a desert and they were concerned about food. The fact that God had powerfully delivered them from slavery and miraculously parted the Red Sea doesn't seem to have made any difference. Instead they complained, "If only we had died by the LORD's hand in Egypt! There we sat around pots of meat and ate all the food we wanted, but *you* [Moses and Aaron] have brought us out into this desert to starve this entire assembly to death" (v. 3, emphasis added).

If you were Moses, how might you have been tempted to respond? I can think of several things I might have been tempted to say. "Seriously, things were better in Egypt where you were slaves?" Or, "If that's what you think, go ahead and go back. I'm not stopping you." Or, "Fine, if you think you can do a better job getting to the Promised Land, go ahead."

Moses didn't make these people his personal enemies. Moses didn't try to defend himself. Moses knew it was God who brought the Israelites out of Egypt and remembered he was God's ambassador. By taking the criticism personally he would have been acting as if "he" had delivered the people from slavery. Moses didn't believe that. He believed God had freed the Israelites, and this influenced his response. Moses went to the Lord and then he went to the people.

Here's what Moses said to the people, "In the evening you will know that it was *the LORD* who brought you out of Egypt, and in the morning you will see the glory of *the LORD*, because he has heard your grumbling against *him*. Who are we, that you should grumble against us?" Moses also said, "You will know that it was *the LORD* when he gives you meat to eat in the evening and all the bread you want in the morning, because he has heard your grumbling against *him*. Who are we? You are not grumbling against us, but against *the LORD*" (Exodus 16:6–8, emphasis added).

Did you notice how Moses reminded the people of God's glory and didn't accept any glory for himself? He even pointed out that their grumbling was against *the Lord*. He also prepped the Israelites to give glory to the Lord, not him, when God blessed them with food.

A proud person in Moses's position would have been devastated, angry, or indecisive. A proud person would have sunk time and resources into trying to figure out how to appease the people and get them on board with his leadership. Knowing that God planned to provide food the next day, a proud person might have just told them food was coming and taken credit for solving the problem. Moses, on the other hand, focused on God's glory and directed the attention of the Israelites to God's glory.

When we meditate on God's glory, a God able to free people from slavery, part the Red Sea, and provide food for two million people in the desert, pursuing our own glory starts to seem ludicrous. It's like showing off our new shoes when we're standing overlooking the Grand Canyon. At that point, our shoes don't seem all that magnificent. There is a bigger glory to enjoy. Moses understood this and he humbly pointed the Israelites to the glory of God.

Drawing attention to God's glory doesn't mean Moses ignored the complaints of the people he was leading. He went to the Lord to ask for help with the real problems that had given opportunity for the complaint. And, just as importantly, when God graciously provided, Moses gave the credit to the Lord. (For other examples of the Hebrews' complaints, see Exodus 5:19–6:9; Exodus 14:11; 15:24; 17:3.)

After we got blamed for something, when it went right, would we give the credit to God or would we let people believe we had been smart enough to come up with a solution? Moses drew attention to God when the people complained to him *and* when the people congratulated him. As you grow in humility, look for opportunities to direct the spotlight to God's glory.

Humble in Victory

Most of us will probably never free a nation of people from slavery. Nevertheless, most of us will probably experience victory at some point and at some level, whether it is raising kids who turn out well, paying off a mortgage, having the best-looking yard on the block, landing a new account, or finding a great sale on an item we wanted. Our investment in the process makes it easy to proudly take credit for the victory. When we do, we are acting like glory thieves. We are exhibiting pride.

This is relatively easy to see in Bryce's desire to have a wife who makes him look good. (Easy for everyone but Bryce to see.) Bryce had nothing to do with Angela's beauty. Angela didn't get her thick dark hair from him. Angela didn't get her beautiful brown eyes from him. Nevertheless, Bryce wants to use these attributes in Angela to glorify himself.

Proudly taking credit for victory would have been an easy line for Moses to cross. Moses had been given the power to perform wonders and the power to bring ten plagues on Egypt to motivate Pharaoh to liberate the Hebrew slaves. Had the situation been a sporting event we might have expected Moses to engage in trash talk with Pharaoh. Had Moses said, "We're going to shatter you. Your mama is going to regret the day you were born." Moses would in fact have been right. It would have been better for Pharaoh to let the Israelites leave immediately. But Pharaoh was a hard, ruthless man and even when the plagues caused him to beg for relief and bargain with Moses, each time he reneged and became more stubborn and angry. Eventually he made a death threat against Moses.

After the final plague when Pharaoh kicked Moses and the Hebrews out of his country, he reneged again. He didn't want to lose two million or so slaves (a conservative estimate of the number of Israelites who left Egypt), so he mustered his army and went in pursuit of them, determined to force the Hebrews back into captivity.

When someone attacks a nation with weapons, we generally call it war. What was the outcome of this war? God drowned Pharaoh and all his army in the Red Sea. What kind of smack talk did Moses spout off after winning a war in which he lost zero fighting men and the enemy was wiped out completely?

Here's an excerpt of what Moses said in Exodus 15:

> "I will sing to the LORD,
> for he is highly exalted.
> The horse and its rider
> he has hurled into the sea." (v. 1)

Moses rightly and humbly exalted God for the victory.

> "The LORD is my strength and my song;
> he has become my salvation.

> He is my God, and I will praise him,
> my father's God, and I will exalt him." (v. 2)

Moses rightly and humbly recognized that God was his strength and salvation and he chose to praise God.

> "Your right hand, O LORD,
> was majestic in power.
> Your right hand, O LORD,
> shattered the enemy." (v. 6)

Moses rightly and humbly acknowledged it was God who defeated Pharaoh. He praised God's power.

> "Who among the gods is like you, O LORD?
> Who is like you—
> majestic in holiness,
> awesome in glory,
> working wonders?" (v. 11)

Moses rightly and humbly gave glory to God. He acknowledged that the victory wasn't due to him; it was all due to God.

When Bryce tries to control Angela or others to make himself look good, he is functioning as if he is responsible for his successes. But humble people understand every good gift is from above. Humble people understand what Paul is saying in 1 Corinthians 4:7:

> For who makes you different from anyone else? What do you have that you did not receive? And if you did receive it, why do you boast as though you did not?

As a result, humble people praise the Lord for his gifts, rather than focusing on themselves. There is nothing wrong with Bryce enjoying Angela's beauty; the problem is that he wants her beauty to glorify himself. Bryce has forgotten that every good gift is from God. Therefore, it is God who should get the glory for these gifts. Do you allow people to believe you are responsible for your skills and successes, or do you draw attention to God? Ask God to give you the grace to draw attention to him with your skills and successes. Try specifically listing how God has used others in your successes.

Moses Didn't Cling to His Importance

Moses responded with grace and mercy to others who threatened his position as leader. Moses didn't try to protect his status.

In Numbers 11, the Lord had Moses install seventy of Israel's elders to help Moses with the burden of leadership. As a sign of their position as assistants to Moses, God enabled the men to prophesy as they were inaugurated.

A couple of the guys invited to join the leadership team decided not to attend the inauguration and stayed home. Basically these guys decided not to follow Moses's leadership. When these guys began prophesying like the other men on the leadership team, Moses's right-hand man, Joshua, exclaimed to Moses that he needed to make the two renegades shut up. Joshua didn't want the community to view these guys as leaders if they weren't going to show up at the inauguration.

Moses's response reflects humility. Rather than saying, "Hey, who do they think they are?" Moses told Joshua he wished the Lord would put his Spirit on everyone (Numbers 11:29). In other words, "I'm not interested in making them shut up—I wish everyone would proclaim words from God!"

Moses didn't consider his position as leader something to be grasped. Moses did what God asks us to do, have the same attitude as our beautiful Savior. Remember that Philippians 2:6–7 explains that Jesus did not consider his equality with God the Father something to be grasped. Instead Jesus made himself nothing. Moses's response shows he was happy for God to be glorified.

Nor did Moses become sinfully angry or vengeful when others wrongfully tried to demote him and promote themselves. In Numbers 12, Moses's sister Miriam got a bee in her bonnet about Moses's wife and spouted off that God spoke through her and her brother Aaron so who did Moses think he was. After God personally rebuked Miriam, he struck her with leprosy. Instead of quietly rejoicing that Miriam got what she deserved for talking about him like that, Moses appealed to God on behalf of his sister. Because Moses didn't focus on his position and his glory, he was free to desire mercy for others. Do you respond with grace and mercy when others don't treat you respectfully? Ask God to help you see the opportunities he gives you to humble yourself. Ask him also to help you consider others better than yourself.

Even When Faced with Great Temptation, Moses Responded Humbly

Perhaps one of the greatest temptations for Moses to become proud occurred in Numbers 14. The Israelites were at the edge of God's Promised Land and most of the scouts sent out to explore the land had come back with a bad report. Despite God's promise that he was giving them the land, these scouts said it couldn't be done.

God responded to the Israelite rejection of him by saying to Moses: "How long will these people treat me with contempt? How long will they refuse to believe in me, in spite of all the miraculous signs I have performed among them? I will strike them down with a plague and destroy them, but I will make *you* into a nation greater and stronger than they" (Numbers 14:11–12, emphasis added).

If God told you he would make you a great nation, how would you respond? Wouldn't it be tempting to say, "Well, if that's what you want, God, go ahead. After all, you are God and you know best."

This was not God's first offer. God had made the offer to Moses once before (Exodus 32:8–14). When God tells you twice that he wants to make you a great nation, surely it's okay to say yes.

Nevertheless, Moses pled with God not to wipe out the Israelites. Why? Because Moses was all about God's glory, not his own glory. Listen to what Moses said to God: "Then the Egyptians will hear about it! By your power you brought these people up from among them. And they will tell the inhabitants of this land about it. They have already heard that you, O Lord, are with these people and that you, O Lord, have been seen face to face, that your cloud stays over them, and that you go before them in a pillar of cloud by day and a pillar of fire by night. If you put these people to death all at one time, the nations who have heard this report about you will say, 'The LORD was not able to bring these people into the land he promised them on oath; so he slaughtered them in the desert'" (Numbers 14:13–16).

Moses was okay with personal disgrace. Moses was okay when people didn't think highly of him. Moses was *not* okay with seeing God's glory tarnished. Moses turned down the promotion God offered him because he was solely focused on God's glory. To be humble we must see life through the lens of God getting the appropriate glory.

For Bryce, faced with the prospect of a dinner with Angela wearing an outfit he doesn't like, seeing the event through the lens of God getting the glory would require a shift in his thinking. First, Bryce would have to make the decision that God's glory is more important to him than his own. This may be more difficult than it sounds. Prying ourselves loose from things that have been very important to us requires the grace of God and the Holy Spirit's gift of repentance. Bryce would need to cry out to God for his help.

Bryce would also need God's wisdom to understand what it is that truly glorifies God. It is not physical attributes that make God look good. His Son had no beauty or majesty to attract us to him; he had nothing in his appearance to make us desire him (Isaiah 53:2). What glorifies God is to love him with all our heart, mind, soul, and strength and to love others as ourselves. We express this love by obeying God and by sacrificially serving others. As we do this, we are conformed to the image of Christ and his glory shines through us.

With this in mind, Bryce could seek to love God and love Angela. Rather than manipulating so that Angela wears the dress he prefers, Bryce could plan how to make the evening enjoyable for her. He could warm up the car so that it's nice and comfortable when Angela gets in. He could thank God for entrusting Angela to him as his wife. He could pray that he and Angela would represent God well to his college buddies and their wives. He could tell Angela how happy he is to have her as his wife. He could give Angela the preferable seat at the restaurant, and he could demonstrate by his attentiveness to her throughout the evening that he considers her a gift from God that he prizes. As Bryce uses God's help and strength to take these steps, God's glory will begin to be seen in him.

The Paradox of Humility

The paradox of humility is that God exalts the humble. God talked to Moses face-to-face as a man to his friend. In Matthew 23:12 we're told, "For whoever exalts himself will be humbled, and whoever humbles himself will be exalted." For those who have lived for praise and glory from others, God makes it clear that he resists the proud. But while he resists the proud, he gives grace to the humble. Thus, as we use God's grace to grow in humility we can expect the abundance of God's grace to be ours. As we clothe ourselves in the King's robes, the glory, honor, and prestige that belong to the Owner of the robe make us look glorious. As we give glory to the King, his glory makes us radiant and, like Moses, we realize we've received a treasure worth more than the riches of Egypt.

CHAPTER 15

Learning to Handle Criticism

"That's not the way to do it. Don't you know how to do anything right? You want everyone to think you're such a good daughter but you're not. If you were a good daughter you would learn how to do this right so I wouldn't have to keep telling you. Get out of here!"

Sylvia leaned against the wall outside her elderly mother's room. This was not the first time her mother had yelled at her, but that didn't mean Sylvia was used to it. Sylvia and her husband had taken her mother into their home two years ago after Sylvia's father died and it became clear that her mother was too frail to live alone. Sylvia's relationship with her mother had never been stellar and so caring for her mom now often felt more like duty than anything else.

Duty was practically Sylvia's middle name. She had an acute sense of right and wrong that guided her decisions and actions. In fact, her desire to do the right thing is what kept her from yelling back at her mom. Her mom's ungratefulness for the sacrifice Sylvia and her husband were making made Sylvia want to lash out, "Can't you see how much we've given up to have you here? You ought to be thankful we've given you a home!"

But Sylvia didn't say that to her mom. Years of keeping quiet when criticized governed her response now. Instead she leaned against the wall, clenching her hands into tight balls, willing herself not to cry. Although she was horrified at the thought, Sylvia longed for the relief she believed would come when her mom died.

Sylvia also longed for her mother's approval. She worked hard to be the best in everything she did and took mistakes very personally. Sylvia interpreted the critical comments her mother handed out so freely as an indictment on her competence and worth. Criticism indicated Sylvia had failed to measure up to the high expectations she lived by. Her mother's constant harping threatened the foundations of Sylvia's goal of living a picture-perfect life.

To an objective bystander, it would be clear that Sylvia's mother bases her criticism on how well Sylvia caters to her selfish desires. As such, it is possible to discount much of her criticism because the source is a quarrelsome old woman who uses her tongue to try to get her way.

But years of enduring her mother's nearly constant barrage of verbal abuse have left Sylvia unable to distinguish between manipulative criticism that is motivated by selfish desires and constructive criticism that is meant for her good. As a result, her husband and children have had to learn to either avoid bringing up issues or to phrase them very carefully so that Sylvia doesn't burst into uncontrollable tears or withdraw into silence. In order to protect herself from the pain of her mother's generally unwarranted criticism, Sylvia has insulated herself against hearing *any* criticism because it has all begun to sound the same to her.

Criticism is hard for anyone to hear. And unfair criticism is doubly hard (although doesn't it all feel unfair when we first hear it?). But for those who want picture-perfect lives, it can be devastating. Yet each of us will encounter criticism in our lives. Is there a way forward that isn't just gritting your teeth or angrily defending yourself?

The Way Forward through Criticism

How do you handle criticism from others? Whether the criticism is fair or unfair (and most is a mixture), it's important to start not with what someone else thinks about you, but what God says is true about you. The truth is that, without Christ, all of us are hopeless cases who deserve God's ultimate critique on our lives. Read what God says about all of us:

> The LORD looks down from heaven
> on the sons of men
> to see if there are any who understand,
> any who seek God.
> All have turned aside,
> they have together become corrupt;
> there is no one who does good,
> not even one. (Psalm 14:2–3)

Left to ourselves, all of us (Sylvia included), are irretrievably broken by sin. Left to ourselves, we don't understand, don't turn toward God, and don't do anything that is good. So, in some sense, the news about who we are is even worse than our harshest critics could imagine. When God looked down on humanity before Christ, he didn't find anyone who truly loved perfection. He didn't find anyone who was good, not even one. Apart from Christ, even when we believe we are pursuing goodness and righteousness, the God of Truth identifies all our self-righteous acts as ultimately being about ourselves—to lift ourselves up, to do good for ourselves, so that we (not God) can be at the center of our world. God sees right through our "good" works. He sees that we love ourselves best. And he calls it like it is—even the good we try to do ends up smelling and looking as bad as dirty rags (Isaiah 64:6).

It might be hard to see how this is a helpful thought when you (or poor Sylvia) are being criticized. But think about it for a moment. God's assessment is the most damning we will ever experience, but the faults he identifies are obliterated when we come to Christ and ask for for-giveness. Unlike those who see just some of your faults and stand in condemnation over you, God sees what you are really like and sent his own Son to pay the price for your sins. God crushed Jesus so your slate could be wiped clean. Now, because Jesus paid for all of your sins, you are free from any condemnation. There is now no more condemnation for those who are in Christ Jesus. And who can condemn those that God accepts (Romans 8:1, 33)? This is grace—amazing and free.

Such grace changes our response to criticism from others. Alfred Poirier points out:

> If I know myself as crucified with Christ, I can now receive another's criticism with this attitude: "You have not discovered a fraction of my guilt. Christ has said more about my sin, my failings, my rebellion and my foolishness than any man can lay against me. I thank you for your corrections. They are a blessing and a kindness to me. For even when they are wrong or misplaced, they remind me of my true faults and sins for which my Lord and Savior paid dearly when he went to the cross for me."[17]

Because Christ redeems you, the criticism you experience can be redeemed by God to be a blessing instead of a curse. Because of God's grace to Sylvia, she can be free from being controlled by her mother's mean words to her. She can decide how to love her mother best, not based on her mother's demands, but on how God is calling her to serve and help someone who is helpless. She can even be free to ask her mother to speak to her differently and then forgive her if her mom's only response is more unkind words. Sylvia can also point out to her mother how much she needs forgiveness and help from Jesus.

God Brings Criticism to Our Attention for Our Good

"Get out of here!" In 2 Samuel 16, David, the anointed king over Israel, receives harsh criticism. A guy named Shimei calls him a murderer and a scoundrel and starts pelting David and everyone around him with rocks. While probably all of us have been criticized, we probably haven't had anyone pitch rocks at us. Nevertheless, wounds received from criticism may be just as painful as being struck by a rock. Few would argue with the truth in James 3:6 that the tongue is a fire. Many of us have been scorched by others' words and sadly, most of us have cut loose with a few scorching words ourselves. We've been on both sides of the equation when it comes to being at fault in our speech. James 3:2 puts it on the table declaring, "If anyone is never at fault in what he says, he is a perfect man." We all know we "fall short" on this one (Romans 3:23).

David's response to Shimei's criticism is unexpected. Remember, David was chosen by God to be king over Israel (1 Samuel 16:12). Knowing that the God of heaven and earth said you were supposed to be king should make you pretty confident when people criticize you. It would be fairly easy to reply, "Look, when God makes you king, you can do things your way. But God didn't make you king, he made me king. So if I were you, I would shut up and get busy paying homage, not throwing rocks and criticizing."

Surprisingly David instructed his people to leave Shimei alone; David didn't have Shimei arrested and shot. This is despite the fact that his five-star general had just volunteered to go take out Shimei. It takes a lot of character to leave someone alone when you've got warriors ready to jump to your defense.

What was going on in David's head to make him respond like that? The Bible tells us that David was thinking that Shimei cursed him because the Lord told him to. David understood that nothing, not even painful criticism, not even criticism that is wrongly motivated and unjust, happens unless God has decreed it (Lamentations 3:37–38). David understood that not one word of criticism could have come from Shimei's mouth unless God had ordained it. So, David told his defenders, "Leave him alone, let him curse, for the Lord has told him to." We don't know all of the reasons that God allowed Shimei to criticize David. But we do know that David was right in thinking that God had a purpose for the criticism.

How about you? Who has the Lord allowed to criticize you? Your mother, your boss, your spouse, your employees, your kids? Why would our good God—the one who loved us so much that he crushed his Son for our failures, the one who promises "no more condemnation"—allow someone to criticize us?

God knows that the answer to this question is important to you. We can't always figure out what God is doing through the hard things in our life, but one thing you can be sure of is that God wants to use difficulties (and criticism is certainly a difficulty) to deepen our relationship with him and deepen our desire for his glory. Because of God's help, Joseph understood this when he told his brothers, "You meant it for evil, but

God meant it for good" in Genesis 50:20. In all things God works for the good of those who love him (Romans 8:28). If criticism can accomplish this in your life, would you consider it worthwhile? Would you consider it worthwhile even if the criticism was wrong and intended to harm you (Genesis 50:20)?

Ask the Lord to See Your Distress and Repay You with Good

Criticism causes distress, and knowing that God can convert it to blessing doesn't mean responding stoically. David told his crew, "It may be that the Lord will see my distress and repay me with good for the cursing I am receiving today." Clearly, Shimei's insults hurt David. David felt distress.

Likewise Sylvia's mom causes distress in Sylvia. It hurts to hear your mother tell you you're worthless when you're trying to do the right thing. Mothers should love their children, not destroy them with their words. Sylvia feels deeply the barbs in her mother's criticism.

Even though Sylvia can't turn to her mother for support and affirmation, she can turn to her heavenly Father. He truly loves her and is able to see her distress and repay her with good. David learned that God is able to see and repay with good long before Shimei started pelting rocks. This was not the first time distress had come to David. As Shimei pitched rocks, David might have flashbacked to his younger days when he often cried to the Lord. Psalm 18 journals one such occasion when David experienced distress.

> In my distress I called to the LORD; I cried to my God for help.
> From his temple he heard my voice;
> my cry came before him, into his ears.
> He parted the heavens and came down;
> dark clouds were under his feet.
> He mounted the cherubim and flew;
> he soared on the wings of the wind.
> He reached down from on high and took hold of me;
> he drew me out of deep waters.

He brought me out into a spacious place:
he rescued me because he delighted in me.
(Psalm 18:6, 9–10, 16, 19)

God had repaid David with good in the past. He had drawn David out of deep waters. He had brought David out into spacious places. David understood that he belonged to a Father who delighted in him and had rescued him many times. When we are criticized we need to remember all of these truths. We too have a heavenly Father who delights in us and rescues us. He doesn't treat us as our sins deserve. We are not being punished by him. He is fitting us for glory. He repays us with good when we turn to him.

As Sylvia turned to her Father, she saw some ways he was repaying her with good even in the midst of her mother's frequent criticism. Her relationship with him became more intimate. Sylvia had a greater appreciation for what Jesus endured when he was despised and rejected (Isaiah 53:3). She started to grasp that God is not like the people around her. People don't show more grace the more others mess up (Romans 5:20). As sin increases, humans show less and less grace. Yet when sin abounds, Sylvia learned that God's grace abounds even more.

Sylvia has also been learning to treasure Christ's righteousness, which is now on her account. Thus, no matter how ugly her mother becomes, Sylvia is comforted by knowing that all of her faults have been dealt with at the cross. Before God she is righteous. And if she is righteous before God, who can condemn her (Romans 8:33–34)?

For Sylvia to think and believe this way is a struggle, since her mother's voice is both loud and frequent, but as Sylvia keeps asking God for help, she is learning to allow criticism to become a path of grace, redemption, and freedom rather than hopelessness, condemnation, and bondage. Sylvia is also beginning to seek help from her husband or a trusted friend when she finds herself confused about what is true about her and what is not. As she has done this she has seen God repay her distress with good, she has experienced healing in the context of relationships that are encouraging and supportive yet also provide constructive criticism.

Welcome the Opportunity to Display More of His Splendor

Often our knee-jerk response to criticism is to assume the other person is completely wrong and to respond defensively. We don't trust God to defend us, so we try to convince our criticizers they are wrong. Think about the cycle this starts: you are told you are wrong; you respond by telling your criticizers they are wrong; they respond by telling you how you are wrong, and so on. In this cycle, criticism never accomplishes anything except stirring up hard feelings.

As one who is a royal heir of God, practice the 1 Corinthians 13 characteristic of love by believing the best about the person who criticizes you. Believe that your criticizer may have observed a blind spot in your life. Trust that your criticizer truly wants to help you change areas that cause your relationships with others to be damaged. Having blind spots uncovered can only help you in your quest to be like Jesus. Accept the possibility that there might be some truth in the criticism you are hearing. Ask the Holy Spirit to search your heart and reveal to you if there are areas where you are wrong (Psalm 139:23–24).

Throughout the Old Testament God repeatedly sent prophets to criticize his people to get them to change course. The Israelites were notorious for being wise in their own eyes even though God sent prophet after prophet to them to tell them they were wrong. Perhaps God is allowing you to hear stinging criticism because you've been blind and deaf. God delights in opening eyes that were blind, allowing people who were in darkness to enjoy his great gifts in the light. It could be that when we receive criticism, God is trying to open our eyes and get us on a right course. Ask God through the Holy Spirit to help you consider the possibility that your criticizer may be right.

Even if very little of what your criticizer says is correct, as is the case with Sylvia's mother's criticism, you can still receive profit and blessing from it. Perfectionists are typically very particular about the details of tasks. "Close is good enough" may work for some people, but this would not generally be true for perfectionists. Perfectionists want things done right. God is also concerned about details, especially the details of our hearts. We see this in passages that instruct us that we must not have even a *hint* of impurity in our lives (Ephesians 5:3) and in passages that tell us that Christ wants us presented to himself without any blemishes or wrinkles (Ephesians 5:27). God cares about details.

Criticism can become an opportunity to iron out wrinkles and remove all traces of impurity. We can mine criticism for gold, looking for the nuggets that will allow us to repent of the smallest hints of impurity in our lives. Even if 95 percent of what we are criticized for is invalid, converting criticism into blessing means we will respond to the 5 percent that is valid with corrective action. The difficult thing here is not to do this with perfectionistic motives that are focused on yourself. Instead, the goal is to open your heart before God and let him sift out all the impurities that no longer belong there. Remembering that you are a child of the King, accepted and beloved, allow yourself to receive correction from whatever source God chooses to use.

"Mine it for gold," Sylvia has begun telling herself when her mother goes into a tirade about Sylvia's faults. "I'm a child of the King, and learning to love my mother despite the constant criticism brings honor to Jesus. What my mother says to get her own way, God can use as a blessing in my life. She may say something that will help me see ways to change so that I can glorify him better and display his splendor more visibly. And even if that doesn't happen, I can bear with her in love and reflect the love of God to those around me." Sylvia has been surprised by the results of listening to criticism with this attitude.

CHAPTER 16

Converting Criticism into Blessing

Let Criticism Reveal What You Value the Most

As Sylvia listened to her mother's constant criticism, she became amazed at how much she wanted the approval of others. Like most manipulators, Sylvia's mom is able to discern small weaknesses in others and then exploit those weaknesses to try to get what she wants. Often Sylvia's mother tries to manipulate her by using Sylvia's desire for approval as a weapon against her. Sylvia noticed that this was often effective because she doesn't want others to think poorly of her. She does want everyone to think she is a good daughter—and not just a good daughter, but a good person.

Faced with the reality that she couldn't convince her own mother that she's a good person, Sylvia was forced to examine herself. She wrestled over whether she would continue to try to convince others she is a good person or whether she would live honestly before others, humbly admitting that she has nothing good to offer in herself and any good in her is a work of God's grace in her life.

This wrestling has been painful but profitable. She hasn't found it easy to live honestly before others, but she is learning the blessings of an authentic lifestyle. As she has given up vigilantly monitoring her approval ratings, the tension Sylvia has been accustomed to living with has begun to dissipate.

Sylvia has started to consciously remind herself that Christ knows all of her sins, failings, and weaknesses, but he calls her his beloved and assures her that he delights in her. Slowly, Sylvia's desire to look good to others is fading; it's being replaced with a growing concern that *God* look good to others—that her life communicates how beautiful he is and that others know the joy of being his beloved.

Sylvia has learned to use criticism as an X-ray into her heart, allowing it to show what she values and desires. Sylvia has converted criticism into blessing by growing in seeking to please God rather than people.

Practice Loving Others as You Have Been Loved

In Sylvia's secret heart, she has looked forward to her mother's death. While Sylvia would never openly admit this, it has been Sylvia's source of hope more and more frequently and she is horrified by it. Perhaps you too have secret hopes that you would never want to come to light. Have you wished that the boss who criticizes you would get transferred or fired? Have you been counting the days until your smart-mouthed child goes to college? Has your response to criticism been to fantasize about a different life, with different people? Has this become your source of hope?

Hope in changed circumstances usually leads to disappointment. Your boss gets transferred, but the new boss is worse. Your child goes to college, but you find you hate being an empty nester. Your mother dies, and you live with intense guilt for harboring a secret longing for her death. Hoping in changed circumstances may not only lead to disappointment, it may result in total hopelessness. If changing circumstances didn't bring positive outcomes, what is left to hope for?

God offers a better hope. "Hope in me," he invites. "Those who hope in me will not be disappointed" (Isaiah 49:23).

Hope in him because his eyes are on those who hope in his unfailing love (Psalm 33:18). He will give new compassions every morning; new compassions to deal with your critical mother, your harsh boss, or your difficult child. The Lord is good to those who hope in him (Lamentations 3:21–25). As with Israel, God's plan is for you to have hope and a future (Jeremiah 29:11). Unlike those who criticize you, God plans to prosper you, not to harm you.

With this hope you can begin to love others as you have been loved by God—with a love that is undeserved, given at a cost, and offered without expected repayment. The offering of this love may take shape in many ways. It may look like:

- Praying that God will pour out blessing on the one who is critical of you.

- Responding with a gentle answer to the criticism. Confessing and seeking forgiveness for the parts of the criticism that are accurate. Asking clarifying questions regarding the parts that don't seem accurate.

- Refusing to retaliate for the hurts you have received. Refraining from gossip and diligently seeking to avoid slandering the one who is critical of you.

- Changing areas that need to be changed instead of stubbornly believing your way is best.

- Speaking kindly to and about the person who is critical of you.

- Thanking the one who criticized you for being bold enough to point out areas that need to be addressed or changed.

- Looking beyond the words to what may have motivated the words and seeking to relieve burdens the one who criticized you may be carrying—burdens such as being stuck in a hospital bed, burdens such as pressure from bosses, burdens such as peer pressure to drink or do drugs, burdens such as a fear of losing one's job, burdens such as home conditions that are difficult and unpleasant, burdens such as a family history of physical and verbal abuse.

These are extraordinary ways to respond to hurtful, critical words. They reflect the love of a Savior who loved us when we were critical enemies of him. When King David was criticized by Shimei, he responded by instructing his troops to leave Shimei alone. David nobly held back the urge to hurt Shimei as Shimei hurt him. In Christ, however, we see a King who not only held back the urge to retaliate against his enemies, we see a King who died for his enemies.

With the help of this King giving you strength, you can convert criticism into blessing by loving others as you have been loved.

Dwell On and Rejoice in What God Did for You through the Cross

Criticism can become an opportunity to rejoice in God's grace poured out on you through the cross. In chapter nine we talked about entering God's courts with thanksgiving and praise. It will be difficult to do this when we've been criticized unless we remind ourselves of Christ's gift of righteousness. Criticism becomes an opportunity to understand more fully what a significant gift Christ's righteousness is. He has done for you what is impossible in and of yourself. You have been gifted with his perfection and, despite the trouble that criticism brings in your life, that is your foundation for a life of joy, hope, and praise.

Augustus M. Toplady penned these words:[18]

> Not the labors of my hands,
> Can fulfill thy law's demands:
> Could my zeal no respite know,
> Could my tears for ever flow;
> All for sin could not atone,
> Thou must save and thou alone.
>
> Nothing in my hand I bring,
> Simply to thy cross I cling:
> Naked come to thee for dress,
> Helpless, look to thee for grace:
> Foul I to the fountain fly,
> Wash me, Savior, or I die.

Wash me, Savior, or I die. This is what Jesus did. He washed you. He turned not only his criticism, but his *condemnation*, of you into your greatest blessing.

With this in mind you can now do what seems unimaginable. You can invite criticism.

Invite Criticism

The psalmist in Psalm 139 says, "Search me and know me, see if there be any wicked way in me" (vv. 23–24). What a radical way to live! The psalmist invites exposure. He is not interested in keeping shameful desires and faults hidden; he asks that they be exposed.

A desire for God's glory cripples a concern for our own glory. As our desire to glorify God grows, we will want to know anything about ourselves that detracts from his glory. It's no longer about making ourselves look good; we want God to look good. And we realize that God does not look good when his children function as if something else or someone else is better or more satisfying than he is—when we act as if we love our mother's, boss', child's, or spouse's approval more than his; when their criticism devastates us but we are unmoved by the ways we neglect our relationship with our heavenly Father; when their commendation creates joy but God's commendation isn't worth working for— we nonverbally declare our allegiance to someone other than God.

But by God's grace our love for him can include a growing willingness to hear from others how we could change and grow. You might begin by asking your spouse or close friend to point out one area in which she would like to see you grow. You may want to preface your request by telling your loved one that with God's help you will seek not to respond defensively to her suggestion, nor will you hold it against her or make her pay for communicating honestly.

If responding well to criticism has been an area that has been particularly difficult for you in the past, you might want to suggest that your loved one begin with something small so that you can approach this task step-by-step. (For example, suggesting you call when you're running behind rather than suggesting you stop being so proud.)

You may find it difficult not to become defensive when your loved one communicates, but resolve ahead of time that you will not say anything to defend yourself. Resolve that unless what is suggested is sinful you will work hard at making the suggested changes even if you don't think the issue is any big deal. Determine that if the criticism is misguided, you will leave it up to God to defend you as he sees fit.

You may need to begin by asking your loved one to tell you about other occasions when she has tried to point out ways to change and you have used it against her. Ask forgiveness from God and your loved one for these times. Chances are she will feel like she is taking a risk to tell you how she believes you could change if you have not responded well in the past. The only way to increase her confidence is to not treat her harshly but with extra kindness and to work hard to implement whatever changes she suggests.

Be Sensitive to Others When You Must Offer Criticism

Finally, convert criticism to blessing by being sensitive to others when you must offer criticism. The lessons you have learned to convert criticism to blessing will have been hard fought and come at a price. You now have the opportunity to bless others by using tender words when you find it necessary to criticize. You know you come as one who is also a sinner, well-deserving of criticism. You know that anything you can find to criticize in another is only a small fraction of the areas for which our Lord could criticize you. Therefore you come tenderly and gently with your criticism, seeking to bind up wounds even as you create them.

As you implement these steps, you will become someone who has learned not only to accept criticism in a mature way but to give criticism in a way that honors Christ as well. Your responses will be a reflection of the response of God to his creatures.

CHAPTER 17

The Weight of Guilt

Kim almost missed the red light ahead and slammed on her brakes at the last minute. She was mulling over the fight she and her daughter Shelby just had as they were discussing plans for Shelby's wedding. Kim wanted the wedding and reception to be picture perfect and she had come up with a guest list of 400 people. Shelby didn't like Kim's plan. Shelby and her fiancé preferred that the ceremony be an intimate family affair, followed by a dinner reception at a local restaurant where Shelby and her fiancé had their first date.

Kim was annoyed. She had invested a significant amount of time coming up with the invitation list and reviewing catering options. She had also put down a deposit on a ballroom at a local historic mansion for the reception and contacted several florists for quotes. All she was asking Shelby to do was tell her what she wanted her wedding colors to be.

But Shelby wasn't on board. She insisted that it was her wedding, and she and Trevor didn't want some big elaborate affair. All Kim's arguments that they needed to invite all their friends and neighbors fell on deaf ears. Kim even quoted the Bible that children are to honor their parents, but Shelby didn't budge. Shelby insisted she wanted a small, private wedding.

Kim knew she'd never be able to look her friends and neighbors in the eye if she did something so shabby. Her friends had all hosted big weddings when their children got married, and they had all invited Kim and her family. Kim was convinced that the people in their social circle would believe she and her husband were too cheap to give their daughter a proper wedding and would feel slighted they had not been invited. Besides that, who had ever heard of a wedding reception at a catfish restaurant?

Kim felt bad often enough about other things; she didn't want to add this to the list. But it was already too late; the fight with her daughter had caused her guilt to kick in. She felt guilty for arguing with her daughter. Perfect moms should be their daughter's best friend, not antagonists. She also felt guilty at the thought of not returning the hospitality of her friends by hosting a big wedding. Why couldn't Shelby just agree?

For many perfectionists, guilt is your unwanted constant companion. No job is ever done well enough—guilt. You procrastinate on important projects—guilt. You sit down to relax for thirty minutes—guilt. You aren't as good a parent as your best friend—guilt. You realize others are upset with you for clinging to your perfectionistic standards—guilt. You don't love God like you should—guilt. Sometimes the guilt you experience is true guilt; sometimes the guilt you experience is "false" guilt.

What Is Guilt?

Kim has been confusing true guilt with false guilt, and this has made it more difficult for her to respond properly when she feels guilty. For her (and us) to be free from guilt, we have to start with a clear understanding of what guilt is. Guilt is the state that occurs whenever we violate God's perfect standard (in other words, we sin) either by *not desiring and doing* what he instructs us to do in his Word or by *desiring and doing* what he instructs us *not* to do in his Word. Notice that sin is not limited to outward actions that are observable to others. Sin is first and foremost a matter of the heart—what we think and desire. The writer of Hebrews admonishes, see to it that you don't have a sinful *heart* (Hebrews 3:12).

Kim is experiencing true guilt for getting sinfully angry with her daughter and arguing with her.

Guilt is often accompanied by bad feelings, but our feelings do not determine whether we are guilty or innocent. It's possible to feel bad when we are doing what is right. When you kindly and patiently correct an underperforming employee, you are not sinning even though you may feel bad. Just because you feel bad doesn't automatically mean you are guilty. Conversely, it's also possible to feel good when we do what is wrong (complaining about an unreasonable boss may make us feel better, getting revenge may feel sweet). Feelings aren't a reliable standard of guilt or innocence. We are guilty whenever we violate God's perfect standard, whether we feel our guilt or not.

Being under the weight of guilt is mentally and physically crushing; guilt robs us of joy and creates a sense of impending doom. Guilt erects a barrier to an intimate relationship with our loving Father. Nevertheless, guilt plays an important role by reminding us of our need for a Savior.

Responding Properly

When we respond to guilt properly, we'll want to praise God. Wait! Where on earth did I get the idea that responding to guilt properly would cause us to want to praise God?

I realized this after reading Psalm 51. King David, a man after God's own heart, wrote this psalm as he dealt with his very real guilt. Take a moment and read it all of the way through. The introduction announces that this is a psalm of David when Nathan the prophet came to him after David had committed adultery with Bathsheba. (See 2 Samuel 11—12 for this account.) Up to that point, David had been covering up; trying to save face; seeking to make sure his guilt was hidden. However, when Nathan came to him, David quit covering; David stopped posing as someone who did things right; David admitted he was far from perfect—he was an adulterer who was so desperate to cover up his guilt that he murdered Bathsheba's husband.

Prior to this, David had been unwilling to admit how badly he had offended God. He had tried to suppress the fact that he had despised

God and his ways and turned to his own way. Therefore, David had lived with guilt as his companion. Guilt comes with many friends, and a boatload had moved in with David—poor health, loss of energy and motivation, feelings of being overwhelmed, depression, anguish, loss of joy, loss of friends, loss of direction and purpose in life, feelings of impending doom, and oppression. David tells us about this in Psalms 32 and 38. When we respond to guilt by trying to cover it up, we'll probably find many of guilt's friends becoming our companions as well.

In Psalm 51, David repents. The word *repent* conveys the idea of turning and going the opposite direction. It connotes doing a complete 180 so that our desires and actions become the opposite of what they were. David demonstrates his repentance in three ways: (1) he admits his guilt (a 180-turn from covering it up); (2) he asks God for mercy and cleansing (a 180-turn from trying to pose as someone who is blameless); (3) he looks to the future and plans to show he's truly repented (a 180-turn from trying to keep his past hidden). Let's look at each of these steps in more detail.

Step 1. David admits his guilt.

In verses 3–6 of Psalm 51, David honestly admits his sin. (Although in this psalm he doesn't state which sin he is confessing, in 2 Samuel 12 he specifically admitted his adultery and murder when Nathan the prophet confronted him.) Step 1 in addressing guilt properly is to agree with God. We have despised God, we have violated his perfect standard, we have chosen to worship another god rather than worshipping the God who paid our ransom and rescued us from darkness and condemnation.

If we are clinging to a desire to have everyone think we are perfect, step 1 will be a stumbling block. Repentance has not occurred. We may feel bad and have some remorse or regret, but we have not repented. We have not turned 180 degrees from our self-focused desires. When self-focused desires rule us, we, like David, are despising God. While we may not have committed physical adultery or murder, we have functioned as if God is of no account, as if we're the glorious ones. We have acted as if this One who loves us with an everlasting love is our pawn, someone we hope to get something from to benefit us. The hip-hop culture popularized the term "player" to mean a man who manipulates women by pretending to care about them, when in reality he is only interested in sex. When we pursue self-focused desires, in a sense we become players with God, pretending to care about him when we're only interested in ourselves.

We're not the first to do this. The Bible records many illustrations besides that of David in which people who belong to the Lord have despised him. Surprisingly, God's compassions never fail. He righteously and truthfully points out that, though he has done great things for us and provided for all our needs, instead of worshipping and praising him we have burdened him with our offenses and wearied him with our sins (Isaiah 43:18–24). Nevertheless, he remains the God who blots out our transgressions by his own choice and remembers our sins no more. He is the Father who welcomes home his prodigal children, not with heavy sighs and reluctant acceptance but with feasting and rejoicing. This is not how we deserve to be treated.

If we have not yet quieted the clamor in our hearts to look good to others and we are reluctant to confess sin because of that desire, then we need to begin by repenting first of our self-centered heart's desires. Remember that God invites us to be stripped of our deceitful desires, to stand naked and bare before him. Not so he can sneer or humiliate, but so we can be clothed with his righteousness. He can purify and redeem our desires and draw us to himself. As God's chosen people, God wants to gift us with a new wardrobe, he wants to replace our proud self-centeredness with a wardrobe of compassion, kindness, humility, gentleness, patience, forgiveness, and love.

Responding to guilt properly requires us to stop being a poser. It requires us to quit trying to convince everyone around us we have it all together. Responding properly means exposing ourselves as a sinner, a failure who is loved and forgiven by God. This doesn't mean we walk around telling everyone all the bad things we've ever done, but it does mean that we confess and repent to the appropriate people. It means we don't pretend not to have any struggles, and we look for opportunities to share with others how God is changing us. Exposing ourselves as a failure who has been loved and forgiven by God draws attention to God and glorifies him. It demonstrates how magnanimous he is. It leads people to regard him highly.

If our sin has been against others as well as God, our confession needs to be as broad and public as the sin. Confessing openly is a pattern throughout God's Word. (See Leviticus 5:5; Numbers 5:5–9; Acts 19:18; James 5:16.) Again, God is magnified when others get to observe how loving he is to forgive sinners. And others can support and encourage us in our repentance.

Step 2. David asks for mercy and cleansing.

The next step in responding to guilt properly is to request God's mercy, compassion, forgiveness, and help (Psalm 51:1–2, 7–12). Being guilty means we deserve whatever punishment is associated with our violation. Prior to salvation this meant we were to be sentenced to death (Romans 6:23). Sinning against God is an automatic sentence to death row. While the Old Testament also spells out specific earthly punishments for sins committed against other people and the New Testament confirms that earthy authorities are to provide punishment for wrongdoing (Romans 13), both the Old and New Testament make it clear that the penalty of sinning against God is death (the soul that sins, it shall die—Ezekiel 18:20) and the wages of sin is death (Romans 6:23, for starters). Without Christ to rescue us by his mercy and sacrifice, we are doomed.

The need for mercy and cleansing doesn't end with salvation however. Although we will no longer face the death penalty from God as Judge, we will need cleansing for the daily sins we commit after salvation. These sins grieve our Father and disrupt our relationship with him. The bottom line is that we still need to be cleansed from the sins we commit after salvation even though the penalty of death has been removed. Jesus explained it to his disciple Peter this way in John 13:10, "A person who has had a bath needs only to wash his feet; his whole body is clean."

When we confess our sins and ask for God's mercy, compassion, forgiveness, and help, God answers yes to that request every single time.

If we confess our sins, God is 100 percent faithful (not unfaithful, not sporadic, not reliable today but unreliable tomorrow) and 100 percent just (not discriminatory, not fraudulent, not vengeful) and will forgive us and purify us 100 percent of the time. Our Redeemer takes our sinful, sorry self and cleanses us.

Step 3. David looks to the future and plans to show he's truly repentant.

Step 3 includes planning what we will do as a result of receiving forgiveness. A good plan includes specific steps to prevent us from repeating our sin and specific steps to show the genuineness of our repentance. In other words, we plan how to reveal how wonderful God is. We plan to glorify God, rather than ourselves. David did this in Psalm 51:13–15.

> Then I will teach transgressors your ways,
> and sinners will turn back to you.
> Save me from bloodguilt, O God,
> the God who saves me,
> and my tongue will sing of your righteousness.
> O Lord, open my lips,
> and my mouth will declare your praise.

In his prayer of confession to God, David lists the things he plans to do after he's been forgiven. Did you notice that David declares he intends to sing of God's righteousness, of God's perfection? David's not interested in making himself look perfect anymore. David's not interested in others seeing him as the king who's got his act together. David's not trying to save face politically. David is all about the perfection of God.

James 5 asks, "Is anyone happy?" and then answers, "Let him sing songs of praise." Forgiveness had made David happy, and he wanted to sing. David wasn't making empty promises when he said he intended to sing of God's righteousness and receiving forgiveness. He not only sang about it, he wrote the song. Psalm 103 records one of his songs, it's a psalm many of us are familiar with.

David begins the song with these words of rejoicing.

> Praise the LORD, O my soul;
> all my inmost being, praise his holy name.

> Praise the LORD, O my soul,
> and forget not all his benefits—
> who forgives all your sins
> and heals all your diseases,
> who redeems your life from the pit
> and crowns you with love and compassion,
> who satisfies your desires with good things
> so that your youth is renewed like the eagle's.
> (Psalm 103:1–5)

David sings about forgiveness. He sings about the love and compassion he has received. From the pit to the heights, forgiveness is sweet. Who wouldn't want to sing?

David ends Psalm 103 on the same high note.

> Praise the LORD, all his works
> everywhere in his dominion.
> Praise the LORD, O my soul. (v. 22)

How close is David's response to your response when you're faced with your guilt and imperfection? Do you follow the three steps David did in Psalm 51?

- Do you admit your guilt?
- Do you request God's mercy, compassion, forgiveness, and help?
- Do you plan to show God's glory as a result of receiving forgiveness? Do you want to sing?

Or, like Kim, do you wallow in the fact that you blew it, feeling miserable and ashamed?

CHAPTER 18

Wallowing and False Guilt

Late that evening, Kim called Shelby to apologize for yelling at her. Kim's apology, as usual, came with a set of excuses for why she had messed up, and Shelby interpreted that to mean that her mom wasn't truly sorry; she just wanted to restore peace and look good again.

Kim didn't feel any better after her apology either. She had beaten herself up for several hours about the fight with Shelby. Why did Shelby always seem to bring out the worst in her? She'd spent hours trying to plan a beautiful wedding for Shelby. Why was she the one feeling guilty? Apologizing left a sour taste in her mouth.

Wallowing in Guilt

Perfectionists often find themselves wallowing in guilt even after they have apologized. Why would we wallow in guilt? There are a number of reasons why this might occur but I think two are especially tempting for the perfectionist.

Reason 1. We've never been taught how to respond when we've been forgiven.

One of the reasons we wallow in guilt is that we've never been taught that the response God wants us to have after we receive forgiveness is joy and happiness. Instead, we believe God wants us to prove how sorry we are by dwelling on our failure and mourning until we think God's satisfied we've been abased enough. While we certainly ought to mourn over our sin, God's really not interested in indefinite mourning. Mourning just puts the focus on us and our sin. Instead the focus needs to be on God and his goodness. This should produce joy. God loves to turn mourning into dancing.

God isn't like a vindictive boss or spouse who wants us to grovel in our misery. God is good. In 2 Corinthians 2:5–9 Paul instructs the Corinthian church to forgive *and* comfort a man who had repented after being disciplined by the church. Paul explains they are to comfort the man so he would not be overwhelmed by excessive sorrow. They were to reaffirm their love for him. By following Paul's instruction, the church would be a picture of how God forgives his children. God isn't interested in having his children wallow in excessive sorrow. Matthew 12:20 tells us, "A bruised reed he will not break, and a smoldering wick he will not snuff out." Instead God takes weak, broken sinners and strengthens them by affirming his love for them. God crowns us with love and compassion.

Although as human beings we may want others to feel sorry for what they did by being sad for a long time, God isn't like that. God is the kind of God who wants us to have joy! Although he would be perfectly just if he wanted the rest of life to be a dirge, God doesn't operate like that. He doesn't hold grudges. On the contrary, he wants us to have joy when we're forgiven. We have a good, kind God.

Therefore, the proper response to God's forgiveness is humility and joy. Don't keep focusing on yourself and your failures because it's not all about you; focus on God and his goodness!

Reason 2. We still want to look good to others.

Kim wallows because in her heart, she is still clinging to the desire to look good. Thus, while she may have honestly admitted to Shelby that her actions were wrong, she is mourning the fact that she's not perfect as she desperately wants to be. Kim hates seeing herself as imperfect. She's embarrassed and ashamed she's done wrong. Her personal glory has been tarnished. And that's why she wallows, because it's about her glory, not God's glory. If it were about God's glory, Kim would be singing his praises for forgiving her yet again. She'd be eager to tell others how to receive the same mercy she's received. She'd be full of joy and a renewed desire to live out her salvation.

Kim lives with an unconfessed desire to have others see her as perfect. This is one of the reasons she finds guilt to be so oppressive even after she apologizes. Kim isn't truly repentant; what she truly wants is to be the heroine whom everyone admires.

Shelby, of course, can see through Kim's façade of perfection. Shelby grew up with Kim and she knows how her mom talks behind people's backs when she is upset with them even though she is nice to their face. Shelby knows how Kim manipulates people with insincere compliments so they will think well of her. Shelby knows that Kim's driving desire is to have others think she is perfect. So when Kim called Shelby to apologize for being snippy to her and fighting with her, Shelby was less than enthusiastic.

There was another reason apologizing didn't bring Kim joy. Kim is still convinced that a proper way to host a wedding is with a big ceremony and an elaborate reception. Even though God has never mandated that parents host elaborate weddings and receptions, in Kim's mind she would be wrong if she did it any other way. But is Kim really guilty before God if she doesn't host all of her friends at a big wedding? Let's look at the difference between real and false guilt.

False Guilt?

To respond to guilt properly, you have to be able to evaluate whether you have violated God's standard. Studying God's Word allows us to know what pleases our Creator. It also informs us what would grieve or displease our Creator. No wonder the psalmist praises God's law in Psalm 19. In Psalm 19:7, the psalmist tells us the law of the Lord is perfect, reviving the soul; not crushing us or grinding us into the dirt.

This should be a relief to a perfectionist. The perfectionist often feels oppressed; her soul needs reviving. Better than CPR to a man experiencing a heart attack, the law of the Lord revives the *soul*. It's bad, sometimes excruciatingly so, to feel bad physically. It's worse to have your soul oppressed. We've all seen people who struggle physically yet seem to have joyous spirits. But if the spirit is oppressed, even good health doesn't compensate.

The weight associated with guilt is crushing. Look at David's description of his guilt in Psalm 38. In verse 4, David says his guilt is a burden too heavy to bear. We've all had things that were just too heavy for us physically, maybe it was a living room sofa or the piano our friend wanted toted into her upstairs apartment; whatever it was, we know about burdens that are too heavy to bear. David makes it clear, that's what guilt does to us; it puts a burden on us that we can't carry. It's too heavy to bear.

Remember we are guilty when we violate God's law. This is important because perfectionists often establish their own law and make it their standard instead of God's Word. Perfectionistic laws might include:

- You should never look sloppy.
- The house should be dusted daily.
- The gas tank should never be below half full.
- Grass clippings must be picked up, not left on the lawn.
- You should host an elaborate ceremony and reception for your child's wedding.

When these "laws" are broken, the perfectionist usually feels bad and labels her feelings "guilt." Let's look at this more closely. Does God's Word command that we should never look sloppy? No. While having a neat appearance may be a nice application of properly stewarding what God has entrusted to us, nevertheless, it is an application, not a law. Therefore, merely having a sloppy appearance does not make one guilty. (Remember, true guilt occurs when we break *God's* standard.)

Similarly, God's Word doesn't command that the house be dusted daily; it doesn't mandate keeping the gas tank half full; and it doesn't prohibit leaving grass clippings on the lawn. While these may be good and appropriate applications of biblical commands and principles in some settings, simple failure to live up to these applications does not make one guilty. Violating God's Word makes one guilty.

Many would label the experience of bad feelings in such situations "false guilt." The term *false guilt* is helpful in indicating that a rule not mandated by God's Word has been established and broken. However, the term is not useful if it causes one to conclude nothing's wrong, there is no problem to be addressed and solved.

In fact, there is a problem to be addressed when "false guilt" occurs. The problem is that of using something as a standard other than God's Word. When "false" guilt occurs, somewhere along the line, the person has begun using someone else's "word" as her standard. Perhaps it's the word of her mother who insisted that the house be vacuumed daily. Perhaps it's the word of a boss who insisted it's not okay to ever make a presentation error. Perhaps it's the word of the dad who insisted it was a sin to be late. Or perhaps it's the "word" of her own heart's craving that she always be the best.

When the word of someone other than God becomes the standard, we become impure and imperfect. Psalm 119:9 asks, "How can a young man keep his way pure?" In other words, how can he live perfectly rather than in an impure and thus imperfect manner? What's the answer? How can we live perfectly?

The answer to living perfectly and purely according to this verse is simply this: Live according to God's Word. By inference, then, living according to any other "word" results in impurity and imperfection.

To the extent that any other standard doesn't line up properly with God's Word we have substituted another "word" for the Word of God and become imperfect and impure. Vacuuming daily was never commanded by God. Thus, to live as if it is wrong to go a day without pulling out the sweeper is to substitute someone else's word for God's. We are to live by every word that proceeds out of God's mouth, not the mouth of someone else. In this case, we are not guilty for failing to vacuum but for failing to use God's Word as the standard.

Thus, while "false guilt" is a helpful term in indicating we have used something other than God's Word as our standard of right or wrong, it would not be completely accurate to assume we are without guilt. In fact, in such cases we would be guilty of substituting some other standard for God's standard. This guilt may have resulted from sheer ignorance of what God's Word says, it may have resulted from being led astray by others who have set up a false standard, it may have resulted from unconsciously thinking that we can make God look good by "adding" to his standards, it may have resulted from an unconfessed desire to appear perfect in the eyes of others, or various other reasons. No matter what the reason, there is genuine guilt to be confessed and repented of.

Coming to God in confession and repentance means those who have been experiencing false guilt will now receive his grace, mercy, and renewed love. His compassions are new every morning (what a good thing since we'll need them renewed regularly). Remember how he wanted the church at Corinth to treat the man who had repented after the church had disciplined him? The church was to forgive and comfort him. This is precisely what God does when you confess and repent. He forgives and he comforts. He gives new joy. He shows mercy afresh. He makes you a useful part of his kingdom. He satisfies your desires with good things.

Kim's struggle with guilt is a struggle with real guilt. Her desire to look good to others by doing the "right" things has led her to stay continually focused on how *she* looks to others. She is consumed with her glory. Thus, it has been a short walk for Kim to begin to set up standards apart from God's Word, standards like what a proper wedding and reception looks like. And so Kim feels guilty when it seems as if she won't be able to live by her standards. She feels as if she will be wrong not to host the wedding she has envisioned. However her guilt is much deeper than Kim realizes. The source of her guilt is a heart that has a sinful desire for her own glory and honor.

As Kim comes to see, understand, and repent of her true guilt, she can begin to know the grace and joy that come from having our guilt removed. She can also begin to retrain her conscience to God's Word, rather than other standards. Kim can sing happy songs. This is a process that will take time. Kim will feel bad for a time when *her* standards are not fulfilled but she can use these as occasions to review the beauty of God's standard, to rejoice in his law, and to live according to his word. By doing this Kim will be retraining her conscience and at some point she can expect the feeling of "false guilt" to stop troubling her.

God will be merciful and kind to Kim in this process. As a father has compassion on his children, so the Lord has compassion on those who fear him for he knows how we are formed, he remembers that we are dust (Psalm 103:13–14). Kim, and all who know what it is to taste God's forgiveness, can sing like David:

> Praise the LORD, all his works
> Everywhere in his dominion.
> Praise the LORD, O my soul.
> (Psalm 103:22)

CHAPTER 19

Never at Rest

As Crystal opened the text from her husband Nathan she already knew what it would be about. Nathan would be texting to let her know he was working late again. Married for a little less than a year, Crystal had been attracted to Nathan because he was a man who got things done. She had dated other men who were full of big talk and big dreams, but Nathan seemed to be someone who made things happen. Crystal had enjoyed Nathan's drive for excellence and had looked forward to their wedding with all the delight and joy one could wish for in a young bride. The wedding had been carefully and elaborately planned, and the framed wedding portraits on the family room mantel were testimony to the couple's desire to have the picture-perfect wedding. Crystal had eagerly looked forward to living happily ever after.

But happily ever after was not what Crystal was feeling now. As a young wife, she was learning that Nathan's drive to accomplish came with negative side effects. Nathan was never at rest. Even when Nathan did come home from work, he didn't rest. When he wasn't checking e-mail and tweaking PowerPoint presentations, he was preparing to teach Sunday school or organizing Red Cross blood drives. Crystal has been trying to figure out why Nathan doesn't seem to enjoy spending time with her. She doesn't understand why all these other things seem so much more important than she is. Crystal feels deserted.

Desertion

Nathan has done more than desert Crystal, he has deserted the gospel. He has deserted Christ. Nathan has begun to pursue a false form of Christianity that presumes to improve on the finished work of Christ. Nathan is not the first to defect.

In the book of Galatians, Paul talks to a church where this had happened. John MacArthur explains,

> Throughout the history of the church some believers have begun well but later have been pulled away from the truths they first believed and followed. They receive the gospel of salvation by grace and live for the Lord in humble faith, but then fall prey to some system of legalism and works righteousness that promises more but produces much less.
>
> Paul had been used [by God to show this church] the truth that salvation is received by faith in Christ's atoning work on the cross plus nothing else. Now they were drifting away from the way of pure grace and had accepted an inferior and impotent substitute based on [laws that] had no power to save. The defecting believers had not lost their salvation, but they had lost the joy and freedom of it and had returned, deceived, to the uncertainty and bondage of self-imposed legalism. They were still in Christ and right with God positionally, but they were not practically living in conformity to the truth by which they had been made righteous.[19]

This self-imposed legalism withholds rest because "cursed is everyone who does not *continue* to do *everything* written in the Book of the Law." No wonder perfectionists like Nathan can't rest. They have to *continue* to do *everything*.[20]

Sadly, no matter how hard you work you will never have done *everything* there is to do. The curse will never go away through your hard work. Doing more will never cause you to feel as if you've done enough. Guilt will always be associated with rest because there will always be more to do if you rely on hard work to meet the requirements of the law.

Unlike Nathan, Christ kept the law perfectly. He did everything and he finished the work. He knew no sin and no deceit was found in his mouth. So when he declared on the cross, "It is finished," he meant it. There is nothing left to be done to earn rest. There is nothing left to be done to remove your guilt and make you righteous. There is no condemnation for those who are in Christ Jesus. Christ took the curse upon himself and he gives you rest.

This changes your labor. Your efforts are not needed to make yourself acceptable to God. When you are in Christ, you are accepted by God through the work of Christ. As a result, your work begins to look different. Paul discusses this in Romans 7:6: "But now, by dying to what once bound us, we have been released from the law so that we serve in the new way of the Spirit, and not in the old way of the written code."

In other words, you will still work and serve but in a new way. Guilt for not doing enough will be replaced with joy that Christ accomplished what you could not do. You can live by faith. Now it's possible to consider resting.

Rest Is Holy

While God commends working diligently and enthusiastically if done from a desire to serve the Lord, God doesn't find it commendable to forego rest. If we are to display his image without distortion, we must rest. God set the pattern for this on the seventh day of creation when he rested from all his labors. In fact, he blessed the seventh day and made it *holy* because on it he rested.

Additionally, the idea of resting was so important to the Lord that rest was included in the top ten list of commands that God gave to Moses on Mount Sinai.

"Remember the Sabbath day by keeping it *holy*. Six days you shall labor and do all your work, but the seventh day is a Sabbath to the LORD your God. On it you shall not do any work, neither you, nor your son or daughter, nor your manservant or maidservant, nor your animals, nor the alien within your gates. For in six days the LORD made the heavens and the earth, the sea, and all that is in them, but he rested on the seventh day. Therefore the LORD blessed the Sabbath day and made it *holy*. (Exodus 20:8–11, emphasis added)

While thoughtful Christians may have differing views on how Exodus 20:8–11 applies to New Testament believers, there can be little question that God is in favor of rest. In Matthew 11:28–29 Jesus says, "Come to me, all you who are weary and burdened, and I will give you rest. Take my yoke upon you and learn from me, for I am gentle and humble in heart, and you will find rest for your souls."

God wants you to have rest. He considers rest a holy thing. You may never have considered rest to be a holy thing. In fact, in your world rest most likely denotes laziness. True, lazy people do profane rest; they take something meant to be holy and set apart for the Lord and use it to satisfy their own selfish desires. In Proverbs 6 the lazy person is contrasted with the hard-working ant, a creature who doesn't have to have a boss standing over it in order to make sure it works diligently. The ant plans ahead and works to store up food for when it will be needed (Proverbs 6:6–8). In stark contrast, the lazy person makes soft little choices—a little sleep, a little slumber, a little folding of the hands to *rest* (Proverbs 6:9–10). The lazy person reasons, there is always "later" to get the work done so why not rest now. The lazy person loves rest, and clearly such rest is not commended in this passage.

However if we are to understand Scripture properly, we must conclude that it is not rest in and of itself that earns the sluggard a rebuke. If that were the case the person who dwells in the shelter of the Most High would be sinful to find rest in God's shadow (Psalm 91:1). Rather, as with all else in life, rest is misused when we try to find it in any source but God alone and use it for any purpose other than his glory.

The writer of Psalm 62 understood this. He both asserts that his soul finds rest in God *alone* (Psalm 62:1) and admonishes himself to find rest in God *alone* (Psalm 62:5). This psalmist understands that rest is all about God, not about us.

The psalmist also shows us that the soul is an integral part of rest. If the soul is not at rest, rest for the body will be profitless.

Souls Not at Rest

The company for which Nathan works is filled with souls not at rest. One of Nathan's colleagues is a man much like Nathan in his abilities and habits. Like Nathan, Ethan also seems to be able to make things happen. Like Nathan, Ethan is also a gifted man, able to excel in a variety of endeavors. However, Ethan doesn't treasure the Giver of all these good gifts. Ethan simply treasures the gift. Ethan has come to idolize the prestige that his talent has brought him and now he is totally invested in making sure he keeps this gift given to him by God. Ethan believes he can maintain and enhance his good reputation and prestige through his unceasing efforts. Ethan is not at rest.

Down the hall, Cecelia lives by the motto that, "If you want something done right, do it yourself." Her trust is in herself alone. Cecelia rarely delegates. Aspiring younger workers hate to work under Cecelia because she is unwilling to train these less skilled employees, preferring to do the work herself rather than risk having it screwed up by a less capable subordinate. Cecelia is not at rest, and the higher the corporate ladder she climbs, the heavier her load becomes.

Two floors down, Levi often works late to try to make up for time lost while he has procrastinated. Fearful that he will fail, Levi regularly puts off his boss's assignments and keeps himself busy with lower priority work. Levi's lack of rest is a vain attempt to do penance for bad choices made earlier.

In the company cafeteria, Billy tiredly swooshes his mop back and forth across a spilled coke. He is frustrated by his boss's expectations. His boss wants to get by with as few employees as possible so he has asked Billy just to spot clean and not spend time cleaning thoroughly. But Billy wants to do his work with excellence and can never be satisfied with the low standards that seem to satisfy his boss.

Nathan's workplace seems full of restless employees. Souls unsettled by anxiety, fear, guilt, and misguided priorities. Souls not at rest.

He Makes Me Lie Down in Green Pastures

In Psalm 23 we see the Lord as a shepherd. In the very first line of this familiar psalm we learn that if we have the Lord as our shepherd we shall not be in want. There is nothing we will be in need of that won't be supplied by the Shepherd. Because the resources of our Shepherd are inexhaustible, we shall *not* be in want. Our anxieties can be retired. We can rest.

But even with this promise some still don't rest. Perhaps that is why in the next verse the Shepherd *makes* us lie down in green pastures. According to Phillip Keller, author of *A Shepherd Looks at Psalm 23*, sheep won't lie down when they are afraid, anxious, or in need.[21] So the way to make them lie down is to remove these threats. This is what our Shepherd does. Our Shepherd says, "Do not fear for I am with you, do not be dismayed for I am your God. I will strengthen you and help you, I will uphold you with my righteous right hand. I will supply all your needs. I am a sun and shield. Don't be anxious about anything, give me all your cares. Nothing is too hard for me. I am a refuge and strong tower. I will protect you."

Nevertheless it sometimes seems our souls have been so damaged by anxiety that we don't rest even though we are in a safe place and have all our needs met. We just don't stop fretting; anxiety has been etched into our souls. And so, we learn in verse 3 that in addition to making us lie down, the Shepherd restores our souls.

God knows a lot about restoring. He is an expert in restoration. He can restore years the locusts have eaten, he can restore fortunes, he can restore jobs, he can restore health, he can restore life, he can restore cities and kingdoms, he can restore joy, he can restore souls. As we dwell on the qualities of our Shepherd and obey his voice, we find our souls being restored. We rest. And as we rest, we are strengthened to fight against the temptation to allow anxiety to rule us. Rest restores our souls and our restored souls enable us to rest. The two go hand in glove. Our Shepherd knows we need rest and he makes us lie down. He doesn't consider rest optional.

CHAPTER 20

Resting

Usually when Crystal gets a text from Nathan that he is working late, she texts back, "What time do you think you'll be home?" This time Crystal texted, "We need to talk. I need help understanding where I fit in your priorities." Wow! Bold text and good question. She was willing to address what Nathan's highest priorities were. Christ too was willing to address priorities.

Martha's Misguided Priorities

Martha, Martha—what thoughts come to mind when you hear those words? For many, what comes to mind is Christ's response to the woman busily trying to show hospitality and get dinner ready for Christ and his disciples while they were in her home (Luke 10:38–42). Hospitality is a good thing, so much so that believers are commanded to practice hospitality several times in the New Testament (Romans 12:13; Hebrews 13:2; 1 Peter 4:9; 3 John 1:8). Yet good things can sometimes take on a life of their own. When this happens we will be worried and distracted. We won't be at rest. Martha had gotten caught in this trap. Christ gently pointed out that her sister Mary had chosen what was better. Mary sat listening at Christ's feet. She was not worried and distracted. She was at rest.

Mary had been able to separate higher priorities from lower priorities on this occasion. But to Martha, getting dinner on the table was top priority. As a result she asked the Lord to intervene and get her some help. She went to the Creator of everything she was trying to prepare and asked him to make her sister help her. It doesn't make much sense, does it? If you were going to ask the Creator to do something, why not just ask him to provide the meal so you could sit at his feet and listen?

It's likely that Martha missed this because she had misplaced priorities. It wasn't as if Martha was doing something bad, the problem was that there was something *better* to do and Martha wasn't doing it. Learning to distinguish good from better, and better from best, is a skill that requires wisdom. When Nathan was organizing blood drives for the Red Cross, he was doing a good thing. However in doing what was good he neglected to serve and honor his wife, a better thing. Does this mean that Nathan should no longer be a Red Cross volunteer? Not necessarily. What it does mean is that Nathan may not serve the Red Cross at the expense of, or in place of, his wife. Nathan's marriage, not his service with the Red Cross, is to be a picture of Christ and his bride. Nathan's marriage is a higher priority than the blood drive.

For Martha, learning from Jesus should have been a higher priority than her meal prep. Again, big elaborate meals are not wrong; God himself has plans to prepare a big elaborate meal for his people (Isaiah 25:6). However we must learn not to sacrifice what is best and settle for only what is good. If we don't grow in this skill we will, like Martha, be distracted and upset, not at rest. If you are not sure how to prioritize your responsibilities and opportunities, seek out wise counsel. Your soul will never be at rest with misplaced priorities.

Rogue Desires

What we desire and want can also sabotage rest for the soul. Desires for the approval of others, for jobs well done, and for a good reputation are spoken of positively in Scripture (Romans 14:18; Colossians 3:23; Proverbs 22:1; 1 Timothy 3:7). They are also all spoken of as having little worth in Scripture (Galatians 1:10; Luke 10:38–42; Philippians 3:3–11). What distinguishes these desires and makes them either good or cheap? I think we find the determining factor in 1 Corinthians 10:31; whatever we do, we are to do it for the glory of the Lord. Whenever this is not the case, we are dealing with rogue desires. Desires that have stepped out of their proper bounds and have become objects of worship. When rogue desires take over, we look to them for life, rather than to God.

Many of the employees at Nathan's company are in the grip of rogue desires. Rogue desires steal peace and rest. They create inner turmoil and dissatisfaction. They stir up anxieties. They stand in the way of rest because achieving them is dependent on you, not on the Lord. These rogue desires are God-replacements. They are things people worship instead of God; things to which people look to for life. You can't go to God and ask him to bless your rogue desires because he's already made it clear he won't give his glory to another. So if you want it, you'll have to look for help somewhere else. And as you know, that's a futile endeavor (Isaiah 16:12). No rest.

"Find rest, O my soul, in God alone" (Psalm 62:5). Not in prestige, not in a job well done, not in the approval of others. There is no rest for the soul apart from God and God alone. The self-existent One, the Creator, the Savior, the Giver of every good gift, the Lover of your soul, the One who is worthy, the Lamb slain for you, the One who lavishes you with love, the One who can't wait to show you the riches of his grace, the One who gives strength to the weary, the One who makes his creatures lie down in green pastures. "A heart at peace gives life to the body" (Proverbs 14:30).

Rest for the Body

Rest is not restricted simply to the soul. The body is also included in resting in God alone. Both soul and body are to have rest. Rest for the body includes rest in the midst of labor and rest from labor.

Rest in labor.

In Matthew 11:28–30 Christ tenderly says, "Come to me, all you who are weary and burdened, and I will give you rest. Take my yoke upon you and learn from me, for I am gentle and humble in heart, and you will find rest for your souls. For my yoke is easy and my burden is light."

If you've ever watched oxen yoked together you know that the yoke is used when there is work to be done, not when the oxen are in their stalls munching on oats. In the same breath that Jesus says he will give rest to all who come to him, he mentions being harnessed into a yoke. Hmm . . . God is not like human beings. When God is in charge and you wear his yoke, even work becomes restful.

If you've ever had a job you truly loved, you can understand this. You didn't have to drag yourself out of bed in the morning because you couldn't wait to get to your job. And even if your job was challenging, you were invigorated by the opportunities, not drained. If you've experienced this, you've had a taste of what it's like to hope in the Lord. Those who hope in the Lord will renew their strength. They will *soar* on wings like eagles; they will *run* and not grow weary, they will *walk* and not be faint. God gives rest in the midst of labor. Running and walking are physical activities and soul and *body* are strengthened when your hope is in the Lord.

Rest from labor.

We would not represent God well if we did not also rest *from* our labor. When God rested on the seventh day, it was his labors from which he rested. So while it is possible to rest *in* our labors, God also established a pattern of resting *from* our labors.

The Old Testament Sabbath was a day set apart to the Lord, a day in which the normal labor required to sustain life was to stop. Fields were not to be planted, crops were not to be harvested, everyone including the animals was to rest and be refreshed.

Planting and harvesting are perhaps the two busiest times of the year for farmers. They spend long days in the field and perhaps it seems obvious they would need rest. However, resting during these seasons requires tremendous trust in God. For example, in harvest when crops are ripe, you generally want to get them in as quickly as possible from the field. You don't want to risk losing them, as fully mature plants start to degrade in quality and are more likely to attract disease and insects. Additionally, a rain at harvest can be expensive, damaging the crop and increasing the harvest costs. As a farmer you want to make hay while the sun shines.

That being the case, resting on a sunny Sabbath no longer makes intuitive sense. It requires deep trust in God and his sovereign control to rest while the sun shines.

In his excellent booklet *Burned Out*, Winston Smith says this, "Resting "forces us to acknowledge that God [is in control]. Resting means acknowledging that our world really belongs to him and we must entrust our well-being into his hands. If you rest for a day, will God keep your life from falling apart?"[22]

Physical rest also requires faith because as David Powlison says, "We live in a 'Go, Go, Go' culture that values achievement and productivity. Rest is not valued unless it's a vacation at an expensive resort."[23]

Perhaps you don't rest because you fear others will believe you are lazy. Living in a culture that values achievement and productivity can easily lead us to the point where we feel guilty enjoying any rest. Yet God gives good things to enjoy, and to snatch moments of rest as though you were doing something illegal is to proclaim to God that he made a mistake in making rest holy. We must properly reflect the Giver in both rest and work, in both body and soul.

Taking Steps to Rest

Nathan was rattled by Crystal's text and forced to do some self-evaluation. The result of this self-examination was conviction and repentance. Nathan realized that resting to God's glory would take deliberate planning on his part. He asked Crystal to help him since he understood that his choices affected her too. Together the two of them made a list of ways to honor God by resting, and they add to it when they see new ways to glorify God in their rest. Nathan now puts scheduled rest times on his calendar to remind himself that both his rest and his labor are valued by God and both reflect the image of his Maker.

Some of the items on Nathan's list are things to *do*; some are things to *think*.

- Devote Sunday mornings to finding rest in the Lord by worshipping him with our local community of believers. Remember that this rest will restore my soul so I can enjoy lying down in green pastures.

- Except for rare occasions, do not engage in the work for which I receive remuneration on Sundays. If it is necessary to deviate from this practice, both Crystal and I must agree that doing so is wise.

- Schedule time weekly specifically devoted to enjoying God's good gifts. This may include going for a walk with Crystal, playing a video game, reading a book and drinking a cup of coffee, etc. Both prior to and at the conclusion of this activity, thank God for the good gifts he gives to enjoy.

- Memorize Isaiah 26:3 as a reminder to trust in God rather than fretting and depending on myself.

- As I pull out of the garage to leave for work each day, remind myself that I am not able to earn any righteousness by my efforts. Christ has finished the work. I am now righteous in his sight, and he is surrounding me with favor (Psalm 5:12). Ask God to help me serve in the new way of the Spirit, not in the old way of the written code (Romans 7:6).

Nathan is still prone to push himself and accept responsibilities that shut out Crystal and preclude rest, but he is taking steps of growth. As Nathan is learning to rest, he has new hope in the Lord. He is finding his strength being renewed as he rests in the God of hope.

Have you sent in your RSVP accepting God's invitation to come to him and find rest? Rest from the clamoring of your soul. Rest from the stresses of modern living. Rest from the burden of sin. Rest from the fatigue of daily cares.

But those who hope in the LORD
will renew their strength.
They will soar on wings like eagles;
they will run and not grow weary,
they will walk and not be faint. (Isaiah 40:31)

"You keep him in perfect peace
whose mind is stayed on you,
because he trusts in you."
— Isaiah 26:3

CHAPTER 21

Evaluations that Lead to Shame

The nurse in Dr. Sanchez's office greeted Mike cheerfully as she escorted him from the waiting room to the exam room. Once in the room, she had Mike roll up his sleeve so she could take his blood pressure. While she did this, the nurse chatted with Mike about the economy and how his company was doing. After finishing the preliminaries, the nurse left the room, pleasantly telling him the doctor would be in, in just a few minutes.

A few minutes wouldn't be long enough for Mike to feel prepared to talk to the doctor about the reason he had made his appointment. This wasn't merely a routine physical. Mike had compared himself to the men he listened to in locker rooms and saw on TV and now waited to tell Dr. Sanchez that he had a problem.

How Are We Doing?

Perfectionists make lots of evaluations. We make these assessments because we want to know how we're doing. Evaluating how we're doing is a right and proper thing to do because God does it. The Bible tells us in Genesis 1 that God evaluated his work regularly during creation; as he finished his creative work he assessed it and was satisfied that it was good. Wanting to know how you're doing is a good thing when done from a heart that desires to glorify God (1 Corinthians 11:31). It's like God, the One whose image you were designed to reflect. However, unlike God, for many perfectionists, the result of their evaluations is far from satisfaction. Rather than looking to God as the standard, perfectionists often compare themselves to others and find themselves sadly lacking.

For perfectionists, the result of their evaluations often sounds like this:

- My colleague had more sales than me this week. I wonder if my boss thinks I'm not working hard enough.
- She never misses any of her son's basketball games. Everyone thinks she's a great mom.
- That couple at church never seem to argue with each other; their marriage seems so much better than ours.
- Mom doesn't visit us as often as she visits my brother. He was always her favorite.
- Ralph's son was accepted at Princeton. I should have made my son take all advanced placement classes this year instead of letting him be in band.
- No one else seems to be struggling; there must be something wrong with me.

Have you had similar thoughts this week when you observed those around you? For many perfectionists, the result of your evaluations may often be shame for not measuring up. With it comes a deep sense that you are unacceptable. Shame then leads to anxiety, envy, discontent, or stress. Other people become competitors in a game of one-upmanship. You live with tension and pressure. You feel naked and exposed.

God's Invitation to Remove Your Shame

Mike wiped his hands on his pants. He felt sweaty and clammy as he uneasily waited for Dr. Sanchez to finish writing his prescription.

According to the doctor, sixty years of demanding living and stress had caught up with Mike. Now here he was getting a prescription for Viagra. All the doctor's platitudes about sixty-year-old men frequently needing a little help in this area didn't make Mike feel any better. From the boasting he heard in the locker room, he knew plenty of other men his age who didn't need drugs. In his mind his manhood came up short. He stuffed the prescription in his pocket and left the physician's office embarrassed and disgraced. He felt like throwing up.

The shame that has swallowed Mike is not unlike the shame many of us feel at the thought of being exposed and found wanting. Mike's shame is intensified because it is associated with one of the most private and intimate areas of his life. Yet shame always makes us feel as if our most intimate disgraces are being or will soon be exposed and made public.

Our experience is a long way from what we hear in Psalm 34:5. In this passage we're told, "Those who look to him are radiant; their faces are never covered with shame." What an astonishing statement. It would seem natural to feel shame with God. Every shameful thing we've ever done is known to God. The humiliating things that we've never told anyone, not even our best friend, are known to God. How could anyone know those things about us and not despise us? How could God know these things and not abhor us? It would seem logical to hide our faces from God—to look down, to look away, to refuse to meet his eyes. Only people who are confident they won't be humiliated look others in the eye. This doesn't make sense.

Go ahead and look. God is not handing down humiliation or scorn; he is handing down grace, mercy, and love. God can be looked at when we're faced with the prospect of shame. Those who look to him are radiant; their faces are never covered with shame. Because Christ bore our shame on the cross and gifts us with his perfect righteousness, we don't have to be covered in shame. If we look to God as our standard of evaluation, not other people, we can become radiant. This can provide the courage we need to trust.

Trust

If we leave Psalm 34 and turn back a few chapters to Psalm 25, we find David facing the prospect of shame. Like you, David dreaded disgrace. David becomes our example of how to look to God.

Psalm 25 begins with David crying out to God. Rather than keeping his fear of shame hidden, as is easy to do when we fear being disgraced, David laid it right out there. David looked to God. David exposed himself. He pled trustingly with God not to let him be put to shame (Psalm 25:1–2).

As we listen to his cry, we hear David telling God that he is baring his soul to him because he trusts him. This trust in God is critical to the process of putting off shame. You must be confident that the one in whom you are confiding won't use your weaknesses against you. Imagine what it might be like for Mike if he told someone who wasn't trustworthy he was taking Viagra. Sly jokes and locker room comments would magnify his disgrace. Removing shame begins with trust, a trust properly placed in God.

Back in Psalm 25, having bared his soul, David reveals why he was willing to be so transparent. David explains his trust. David was willing to be open about his fear of being shamed because he had confidence that no one whose hope is in the Lord would *ever* be put to shame (Psalm 25:3). Ever? Not even when you have to walk into a pharmacy and have a Viagra prescription filled? Not even when you come up short as a parent, spouse, friend, or employee? Not even when you're struggling and no one else is? How could David be so convinced that God wouldn't let him be put to shame? How could David be so transparent? Why was David so confident?

David's hope sprang from his familiarity with God's character. First, David knew God is willing to help *everyone* who hopes in him. There is *no one* who hopes in God who will ever be put to shame. If we are to put our hope in God, knowing that God will never exclude us is crucial (Psalm 25:3). There would be little point in pinning our hopes on God if we thought he would turn his back on us. Perhaps you know what it's like to depend on someone to come through for you only to have them desert you. Perhaps it was your partners for the group project worth 50 percent of your grade in a required college class; or your boyfriend or girlfriend—the one you thought you were going to marry; or your dad who assured you he'd be at your game; or your boss who promised you a promotion. Dashed hopes. Broken confidences. Shattered trust. But *no one* who trusts in God will *ever* be disappointed. Never. Not once. Not ever.

Skeletons in the Closet

Even as he expressed confidence that he wouldn't be put to shame, the skeletons in David's closet weren't far from his memory. He was plagued with internal doubts as he recalled former sins (Psalm 25:7, 11). Yet David knew God is merciful and loving. Even though shame would be a well-deserved consequence of former sins, David would not get what he deserved. He would receive mercy from the hand of a loving God (Psalm 25:6–7). Mike too will receive tenderness from God. Even though he has poked fun at men in Viagra commercials, Mike will not receive ridicule from God. He will not get what he deserves. He will receive mercy.

God doesn't top out at granting mercy; he opens the vault and brings out the trade secrets. He *confides* in those to whom he has granted mercy; he shows them his perfect ways. God mentors those who have messed up and he guides them in the right way (Psalm 25:8–9, 12, 14). He guides them in *his* way. Nor will God change his mind and withdraw his help. God won't get mad, take his toys, and go home. God is loving and faithful (Psalm 25:10, 21).

Our Responsibility

But just knowing these things about God is not enough. Psalm 25 indicates David recognized that in order not to be put to shame, he had responsibility.

Hope in God.

First, David understood he must put his hope in God (Psalm 25:3); his hope had to be in God's perfection, not his own. Hoping to avoid shame by trusting in our own works of perfection leads to embarrassment, disgrace, and humiliation. Whereas Mike could once crudely joke and boast about sex in the men's locker room, he can't do that anymore. Men taking Viagra don't boast about what happens in bedrooms. God has stepped in to get Mike's attention. God will fight for your attention as well. God will allow someone else to come up with a better marketing plan, he will allow your brownies to be dry, he will allow your deadline to be missed. He will not let you repeatedly have credit for his good gifts; he will not give his glory to another. Our hope must be in Christ's perfection.

Freedom from shame is not something we deserve. Freedom from shame demonstrates God's mercy, a rich and abundant gift in which God cleanses miserable failures and clothes them in his royal robes. He allows his glory to settle on us through the work of Christ.

Follow and obey God.

Wearing the robe comes with royal responsibility. David recognized his responsibility was to follow and obey God (Psalm 25:10). It is God who is the boss and king. Although he was a king, David was not the ruler who told his servant God what to do. God is the master, and David was to be his obedient servant. David was to submit himself to God, not function as a rebellious son who wants to take over the throne from his father.

Mike may want to acknowledge his willingness to follow and obey by praying something such as, "Lord, you are the King of the universe. I praise you for your sovereignty. Thank you for your rule, not only of the universe, but in my life as well. This prescription, Lord, is not what I would have chosen had I been king of the universe. I thank you that you are all wise and knew exactly what I needed to mold me into the likeness of Jesus. I am tempted to focus on the embarrassment I feel, but with your help, I will instead focus on your great power and love.

"I know that your purpose in this is to help me grow in loving you and loving others. Because of this circumstance in my life, you have opened my eyes to how much I've been concerned about my honor and my reputation. I've realized that one of the reasons this is so humiliating to me is because I have had a proud attitude. Will you please forgive me? Will you please show mercy to me yet again?

"Then, Lord, please help me to follow and obey you by loving others. Instead of continuously monitoring what others think of me, help me to monitor whether I am serving them.

"Please help me! I love you! I'm glad you're the King."

Fear the Lord.

It was also David's responsibility to have a deep awe (fear) of the Lord, not other people (Psalm 25:12, 14). If either Mike or David were to give their fear and awe to people and to use others as their standard of evaluation rather than the Lord, shame would always lurk in the corners. There will be many people who are not merciful, loving, or willing to confide how to achieve success (Psalm 25:3). Rather they will be delighted to put everyone around them to shame to make themselves look good.

David knew this was not an area in which he could ease up and be less than vigilant. He had to stay focused on the Lord, not on other people and their evaluations and opinions. Were he to become lax in this regard, shame would instantly engulf him. David expressed his conviction like this: "My eyes are *ever* on the LORD, for only he will release my feet from the snare" (Psalm 25:15, emphasis added). Only by keeping his eyes on God would he be free of shame.

Take refuge in the Lord.

Finally, David had the responsibility to trust in the Lord and take refuge in him (Psalm 25:1, 15, 20). It is those who trust in the Lord who will not be put to shame. God alone can prevent shame from overtaking you. David had to take cover in the Lord. But taking cover in the Lord doesn't mean hiding in some hole in the ground hoping your enemies won't find you. Hiding in the Lord allows you to live openly because there is no need to fear that exposure will ruin you. You have already been exposed by the Lord and cleansed. Now you are protected by the King and you wear his robe.

Some Steps to Consider

As you run to God for refuge, here are some steps to help:

- Trust God. Believe and act on your certainty that God is who he says he is.
- Cry out to God. Humbly ask him for help.
- Bare your soul to God. Tell him your fears, your struggles, your shames.
- Ask God not to let you be put to shame.
- Rely on the fact that the way not to be shamed is to trust God.
- Determine to get to know God better. (You can do this daily by studying his Word and putting it into practice.) He wants to confide in you. He wants to show you the joys of being his heir.
- Rejoice that God wants you to know him. He won't blow you off like someone who lost interest in you after a few dates.
- Rejoice that God has a vested interest in you. He is your Savior.
- Rejoice that your sins have been removed and that you are loved and accepted by God.
- Be willing to do things God's way. Don't insist that your way is best.
- Don't be surprised if you still struggle with distress. Continue to hope in God—confident that those who look to him are radiant. Their faces are never covered with shame.

For Mike, leaving his doctor's office with a prescription in his pocket for a drug he never wanted to take, Psalm 25 can help prevent him from responding in pride, fear, and anxiety. Rather than living with desperation, Mike can look to God to be free from shame.

As time has passed, Mike's circumstances have not changed. He is still a man with a Viagra prescription. However, change is taking place in Mike's life. As he trusts in the Lord, his life is defined less and less by his comparisons with others. As he focuses on what it means to be in Christ, he is becoming acquainted with the joy of belonging to a good God. Mike doesn't have depression, bitterness, or anger etched into his face. His circumstances have not made him sour. Mike is staking everything he has on God and he knows he won't be disappointed or abandoned by him.

This confidence has had to be worked out in Mike's life. It is not something that occurred automatically. Rather it is something that required deep trust and perseverance on Mike's part. Rather than seeing every other man as a competitor whom he wants to beat, Mike has had to train himself not to treat other men as foes but as either fellow royal heirs of God's kingdom or persons living in darkness in need of grace.

Wrestling to take captive each thought when he is tempted to measure his manhood against other men has been difficult, but it has produced a perseverance in Mike that has led to character. There is now a quiet hope in Mike that sets him apart from men whose comparisons lead them to shame. This hope was what caused Trent, a younger man in Mike's church, to seek Mike out to mentor him.

For the Mikes of this world, satisfaction is not found in locker room comparisons. Manhood is no longer defined by sexual prowess at age sixty. Delight comes in the Lord, in wearing his royal robe, in sharing in his righteousness, in the beauty of his perfection. And when the source of delight is the Lord, comparisons to others become weak and impotent to create shame.

> He will spend his days in prosperity,
> and his descendants will inherit the land.
> (Psalm 25:13)

CHAPTER 22

And When We Fail

Mike's daughter Laura was in town visiting with her children and this afternoon Mike had taken Laura and the kids to an ice skating rink the kids had been eager to visit. Mike watched as the kids begged their mom to join them on the ice.

However Laura didn't know how to skate and the rink was crowded with skaters. Laura had no desire to get out on the ice and make a fool of herself. "I told you this would happen," Laura moaned to Mike.

But Laura was too soft-hearted to ignore the pleas of her children and reluctantly she rented a pair of skates. With Mike's encouragement and her children, Madison and Asher, supporting her on either side, Laura took her first tentative steps on the ice. Not surprisingly, it wasn't long before Laura also took her first tumble. After four more falls, Laura was ready to quit.

Ice skating is not the only endeavor where Laura has been tempted to quit. Laura tends to become discouraged quickly after failure.

"I quit. I just can't do this! This is too hard." How many times have you thought or said this after you've tried something and failed? If you are a perfectionist, more than likely you want to do it right or not do it. You don't attempt things if you think you'll fail. Once we despair, quitting seems to be the only reasonable option. If we can't succeed, why waste time and emotion trying if we're only going to fail? This is where Laura has landed.

Proverbs 24:16 tells us that a righteous man falls seven times but he rises again. Thus, as God's royal, righteous children, not just Laura but all of us have the option to keep going. It may take us awhile to get it right (the righteous man falls seven times), but we can learn from each failure and rise again and again and again and again and again and again and again.

Let Perseverance Finish Its Work

James 1:2–4 says,

> Consider it pure joy, my brothers, whenever you face trials of many kinds, because you know that the testing of your faith develops perseverance. Perseverance must finish its work so that you may be mature and complete, not lacking anything.

Notice that the words *mature* and *complete* are used to describe the outcome of persevering under trial. Failure is one of the many kinds of trials God can use to help us grow in maturity. There are lots of worldly examples of folks who persevered after failure and are considered successes, for example, Thomas Edison who made 1,000 unsuccessful attempts at inventing the lightbulb, Walt Disney who was fired by a newspaper editor because he "lacked imagination and had no good ideas," and Michael Jordan who didn't make his high school varsity basketball team when he tried out as a sophomore. Imagine what God wants to do when it's one of his children who doesn't quit because she wants her Father to be glorified.

If God will honor perseverance in folks with lesser motives, what must he be willing and wanting to do when the motive is to be like Christ! Persevere. Be steadfast. This opportunity is being used by God to conform you into the image of Christ. From God's hand to your hand, the very thing you've longed for is being offered to you by God. Accept the gift he is offering by rising again.

The character of the perfectionist is often described using some of these bullet points we saw in chapter 1:

- You want to be the best in everything you do.
- You have very high expectations for yourself and others.
- You are very upset with yourself if you make a mistake.
- You feel guilty for relaxing. You feel like you are never doing enough.
- You're very particular about the details of tasks.
- When you perform well, you analyze your performance for the weak spots and quickly gloss over the things done right.
- You want something done right or not done at all.
- You compare yourself to others. If you perceive someone is better than you, you analyze that person to see how to measure up.
- You don't attempt things you know you can't complete with excellence.
- You are frightened by the thought of failure.
- You procrastinate.

However, as you persevere, a new character can be formed in you. This new character might have the following bullet points to describe it:

- You love the Lord fervently and regard him as the best thing that ever happened to you. You want others to see just how magnificent he is.
- You are humbly in awe that all the perfection and righteousness you were working to achieve has been gifted to you by Christ. You expect to follow hard after him all the days of your life and encourage others to do so as well—strengthening them when they falter.
- You mourn when you sin and quickly run to your Father to express sorrow over your sin, receive his forgiveness, and then press on with renewed joy.
- You praise God that he has granted you rest—rest from being his enemy, rest from striving to achieve righteousness through your own works, rest from the burden of sin, rest from the

belief that he will be displeased if you relax and enjoy his good gifts, and rest from the oppressiveness of living in a fallen world.

- You have turned your attention to detail onto your heart. You can never be satisfied with even the smallest vestige of sin residing in your heart. You plead with God to search you and know you and then to show you if there is *any* wicked way in you so that by God's grace and through the empowerment of the Holy Spirit you can repent and mercilessly uproot it.

- When you perform well, you praise God for his work through you. You spend significant time in worship praising your marvelous Savior in great detail for the work he has done.

- You continue to want things done right so long as right is defined as bringing glory to your Savior. You have become wise enough to know that you and others may take many faltering steps in this process, and you are willing to invest as much time and effort as it takes to move toward Christ's likeness. You are willing to rise again after each fall and to extend a hand to others when they fall repeatedly to help them rise again also.

- Your only point of comparison is now your Savior. You thirst to be like him. You long to reflect his image. You continuously compare yourself to him, rejoicing as you see maturity occurring as well as mourning when you see you haven't treasured being like him.

- You have the boldness and confidence to attempt anything that would glorify God. You are convinced that if your desire is to glorify God, you will be granted the blessing of bringing glory to him.

- You are emboldened by a Spirit of love rather than frightened by the thought of failure. You know the Mighty One and your fears are quieted by his love. You search out ways to show others the same love you have received.

- You diligently determine the "next right thing" to do and faithfully perform it even if you're not sure how to do the entire project. You are not foolhardy or careless, but you are eager to see what God is up to. You hasten and do not delay to keep his commandments (Psalm 119:60).

Don't Focus on Hiding Your Flaws, Instead Show God's Glory

> The LORD upholds all those who fall
> and lifts up all who are bowed down.
> (Psalm 145:14)

God seems to take delight in picking people up after failure. On more than one occasion Abraham lied to important people, yet God called Abraham his friend. Moses committed murder, but God used him to free a nation of people from slavery. David committed adultery and murder, but God didn't pull away from him. David is later called a man after God's own heart. (Would you use people like this to make you look good? Would you give them the job of reflecting your glory?)

Let people see how glorious God is by letting them see your failures. When you are transparent about your failures, you promote God's glory. Our failures allow God to display his faithful and merciful love. Failures allow God's power to be put on display. Failures allow God to prove that he is as forgiving as he says he is. So consider being open and transparent about your failures in order to show God's glory.

Often perfectionists are extremely reluctant to do this. We want others to think we have our act together. We don't want others to know how we fail. We want our failures to be kept hidden. But hiding our failures doesn't show God's mercy and long-suffering.

This testimony from a graduate of a residential treatment program demonstrates how Jesus is magnified when we don't try to hide our failures.

> I am free to admit I am human and sinful because guilt and con-demnation are not mine. It is not my record that I look to to save my life. Christ's sacrifice is enough for everything I have done and will do. And God can use what was once my rebellion and shame to show the overwhelming bigness of his grace. Sin can seem so overwhelming and big . . . but grace is bigger and deeper, and it is God's pleasure to reach people in dark places and make their lives to the glory of his name. It's a relief that my

salvation is God's work . . . that it is up to him to save and keep me. If my life is about showcasing the gospel then it is to my advantage to say I am wicked . . . in my flesh there is nothing good . . . and even to share [how I've failed]. The beautiful thing is that Christ wanted me anyway, because he came to find and save those who were sick in sin, and I am freed from living as prisoner to the shameful life I created for myself, and given the ability to pursue Christ and become like him.[24]

When we're willing to openly acknowledge we are failures, God's marvelous work of redemption can be brilliantly displayed and serve as a source of hope for others. So rise again by being transparent. Allow God's greatness to be displayed through his forgiveness and restoration in your life. Say with the psalmist of Psalm 66:

> Come and listen, all you who fear God;
> let me tell you what he has done for me. (Psalm 66:16)

Is It Ever Okay to Quit When I Experience Failure?

With these reasons to rise again, is it ever okay to quit? Is it ever okay for people like Laura to determine they are done trying to ice skate? Can we resign or hand projects off to someone else?

Yes, we're often free to quit. But what is permissible is not necessarily our most noble choice. In 1 Corinthians 10 Paul reminded believers to use their freedom for God's glory. Paul said, "Everything is permissible, but not everything is beneficial" (v. 23). Paul insisted that freedom be used to glorify God (1 Corinthians 10:31). Therefore, the option to quit should generally be exercised infrequently, with great reluctance, and after receiving counsel from those who can give wise input. In Galatians 6:9, God encourages us not to become weary in doing good. In other words, don't quit. In Hebrews 12, God tells us to run with perseverance. In other words, don't quit. In James 1 we learn that perseverance must finish its work so that we can be mature and complete. In other words, don't quit.

When tempted to quit, it's probably best to ask ourselves some heart questions.

- Do I want to quit because this is hard?
- Do I want to quit because I'm embarrassed?
- Do I want to quit because I'm discouraged?
- How will quitting help me bring glory to God?
- How will quitting help me to love others?

Clearly when something is sinful we should quit immediately. But in other cases we need to carefully consider if failing to persevere will short-circuit our growth and maturity. I think it's probably safe to say that generally God will receive more glory if you don't quit. So, the bottom line is this—unless it's sinful to continue, be very slow to quit. Do it with great reluctance. Be quick to persevere and slow to quit.

Happily Ever After?

Did you notice that none of the people to whom you've been introduced in this book had stories that ended with "and they lived happily ever after"? That's because our growth won't be complete until we finally get to be in God's presence with our beloved and adored Father and Savior. That's when happily ever after begins.

So for perfectionists and nonperfectionists there is still work to be done. The coursework of suffering, discipline, and praise that we discussed in earlier chapters has not been completed. We all need to take continued steps of growth. At times it will probably seem as if we are in reverse but we can be confident that he who began a good work in us will carry it on to completion.

What will completion look like? It will look like Jesus Christ! At the end of God's good work in us, we will be completely conformed to the image of our Savior and we will reflect his glory brilliantly.

Along the way there will be defeats and victories, all overseen by the God who loves us, who cares for us deeply, and who died a horrific death to make us his. As a result we can have confidence and joy. We can persevere in God's school of growth. We can know the grace of God, we can rejoice in the grace of God, and we can offer his grace to others with the same kindness and love with which he offered it to us.

As you continue to grow you should expect to see yourself become more loving, more joyful, more confident, more patient, more bold, more gentle, more kind, more self-controlled, more humble—more like Christ. You should also expect to be less satisfied with and more aware of how infinitely far you fall short of the perfect standard of Christ. As you fall and rise, it may be easy to only see the scabs on your scraped knee, but as you persevere, what others will see is more and more of Christ. Yes, this is a difficult process but, like Moses, Paul, Abraham, and countless others before you, you can fix your eyes on Jesus and run toward the prize—toward the treasure and riches found in our Savior.

So don't become weary in your well doing. A beautiful harvest awaits. You can become a royal heir who radiates your Savior. And you can grow in maturity, content to be in the growth process, and looking forward to its perfect completion when you are with Christ.

Discussion Questions

Chapter 1 I Love Perfection! I Hate Perfection!

1. Do you have a love/hate relationship with perfectionism? What do you love about it? What do you hate?

2. Which of the perfectionist's trademark characteristics tend to be true of you?

3. How could the better way Christ offers make your life different?

Chapter 2 Ian: Performance-Based Perfection

1. As you look at your life, have you found that, like Ian, a desire for perfection both draws and repels you? Give some examples of ways you've found this to be true.

2. What benefits have you hoped to achieve through perfection?

3. What are the things you hope perfection will protect you from?

4. What is your understanding of the better way Christ offers?

Chapter 3 Linda: The Angry Mother-in-Law

1. Do you have demands God hasn't met? What are they? (Hint: try thinking about areas where you are frequently frustrated.)

2. What truths would help you not to be drawn into the trap of performance-based perfection?

3. Why shouldn't we just "let go and let God"?

Chapter 4 Harmony: A Father Who Can't Be Pleased

1. Do you use perfectionism to gain the approval of others? List the people you would especially like to receive approval from.

2. What should be our *only* reason for longing for perfection? Why?

3. Do you believe you can please God? How and why?

4. Give some examples of times you've relied on God's grace to glorify him. Was God pleased? Were you pleased?

Chapter 5 Greg: The Defeated Perfectionist

1. Are there areas in your life in which you've given up? Why did you give up?

2. How do you usually deal with shame?

3. Go back through the gifts and privileges for those who have the righteousness of Christ on their account. Instead of "you," substitute "I" or "me." What reaction did this stir up in you?

Chapter 6 Penny: "Living for Jesus"

1. Can you see ways that you've slipped into "living for Jesus" and been busy doing godly things from a heart focused on yourself? What does this look like in your life?

2. How would you describe your intimacy and relationship with the Lord?

3. Can you see ways you are like Ian, Linda, Harmony, and Greg? What are they?

4. Reread the bulleted list on page 58. Specifically praise God for each of these things.

Chapter 7 A Perfect Standard

1. What is your response to Christ's instruction to be perfect as your heavenly Father is perfect?

2. What was Jesus's purpose in making the standard of perfection God himself?

3. As you examine the "fruit" in your life, what do you find?

Chapter 8 Growing into Our Position

1. What is your attitude toward growth in the likeness of Christ? Are you satisfied or dissatisfied in being a dependent child? Why?

2. What has your typical view of and response to suffering been like? Do you find it surprising that Christ was made perfect through suffering and that we are to consider suffering pure joy?

3. What heart desires has suffering exposed in your life?

Chapter 9 More Classes in God's Academy

1. Read Ephesians 4:20–24. What three-step method is described to help you grow? Use these three steps to specifically describe how you can grow in one area of your life.

2. Read Psalm 100. Spend some time simply expressing praise to God. Perhaps you would enjoy thinking of an attribute of God for each letter of the alphabet and praising him for these character traits.

3. Describe one area in your life in which you can look back and see God's grace producing growth and maturity.

4. Try asking someone who has known you a long time to tell you how they have seen you change. Consider asking them to name one thing about you they would change if they could. If they are willing to take the risk to tell you, you might want to jointly work through Ephesians 4:20–24 to create a specific plan for growth in that area.

Chapter 10 Satisfaction that Lasts More than a Moment

1. List some examples of ways you've seen God use his sovereignty for your good this past week.

2. Look at your schedule and survey how much weight is being given to the various areas God has entrusted to your stewardship. What does your schedule reveal?

3. Do you have examples from this past week where you stopped "perfecting" one area in order not to neglect other areas of stewardship God has entrusted to you? What are some of your examples?

Chapter 11 Paralyzed by Fear

1. Describe how fear of failure affects your life.

2. Describe two recent situations in which you followed Jehoshaphat's process described in the bulleted points on page 103. What was the outcome in those situations?

3. Describe a recent situation when you didn't depend on the Lord? What was the outcome?

Chapter 12 A Spirit of Power, Love, and Self-Control Instead of the Paralysis of Fear

1. What standard do you tend to use to evaluate success and failure? Give an example of a time you were successful according to God's standard.

2. Describe three opportunities God has given you to smother fear with love.

3. Are there projects in your life for which you need to exercise the spirit of self-control God has gifted to you and do the next right thing? What is the next right thing?

Chapter 13 Bryce and Angela: Two Ways of Trying to Look Good to Others

1. Do you have people in your life whom you consciously or unconsciously expect to bring you glory (children, spouse, employees, friends)? Who are they?

2. Do you fear not looking good to others? How does this show up in your actions?

3. Consider the following characteristics of proud people. Which ones do you tend to find in your own heart?

• Proud people want to do and be better than others.

• Proud people never want to fail or look bad to others.

- Proud people worry about what others will think of them.

- Proud people don't admit where they struggle because they want to look good to others.

- Proud people judge others who don't live by their standards.

- Proud people add to God's standards. They set their standards up as better than God. (House should always be perfect.) Proud people insist on their own standards.

- Proud people seek honor for themselves.

- Proud people think they shouldn't have to fail or struggle with sin for a long time. They think they are different from others.

- Proud people act as though they are responsible for the things they have, instead of acknowledging they are from God.

- Proud people grumble and complain. (Potatoes too brown.) Pride finds fault.

- Proud people love to be first. They are number 1.

- Proud people put a greater dependence on themselves than dependence on God's grace and provision.

- Proud people resort to defensiveness, blame shifting, justification, or anger when criticized by another.

- Proud people invest more resources to establish their own honor than God's honor.

- Proud people are ungrateful for God's mercies.

- Proud people have an inability to see their own sin or to recognize the magnitude of it.

4. Do you make self-deprecating comments? If so, list a couple you have made recently and ask yourself the bulleted questions on page 119.

Chapter 14 Lessons from a Humble Man

1. Moses regarded disgrace for the sake of Christ as of greater value than the treasures of Egypt. What do you treasure? Do you struggle with treasuring the high regard of others more than your identity in Christ? If this is the case, have you cried out to God for help?

2. Describe three recent times when you've been able to direct the spotlight to God's glory.

3. Give four examples of ways God has used others in your successes.

Chapter 15 Learning to Handle Criticism

1. Who has criticized you recently? How have you responded to their criticism?

2. How could the quote by Alfred Poirier help you when you receive criticism?

3. Give an example of a nugget of gold you've received from criticism.

Chapter 16 Converting Criticism into Blessing

1. What are some of the helpful things you've learned from receiving criticism in the past?

2. Describe four ways that you have shown love to someone who has been harshly critical of you.

3. Consider praying and asking God to allow someone to criticize you this week for your benefit. How should you prepare for this?

4. Read Luke 7:36–50. Do you think the Pharisee's criticism mattered to this woman? Why?

Chapter 17 The Weight of Guilt

1. In what areas in your life do you tend to feel recurring guilt?

2. Cry out to God in prayer regarding the areas you listed in question 1. Follow David's example by (1) admitting your guilt, (2) asking God for mercy and cleansing, and (3) making plans to demonstrate repentance. What happened when you did this?

3. Do you praise God after you receive forgiveness? Try praising God by loudly reading Psalm 103.

Chapter 18 Wallowing and False Guilt

1. Do you find yourself tempted to wallow in guilt when you mess up? Why do you think you are tempted to respond this way?

2. Make a list of standards you've established that are very important to you but are not God's laws. How does your conscience respond when these standards are broken?

3. Is the concept of "false guilt" presented in this chapter new to you? Explain in your own words what it means.

Chapter 19 Never at Rest

1. What attitude have you had toward rest? Does your attitude reflect God's attitude? How are they alike or different?

2. What things in your life tend to sabotage rest?

3. Can you see any evidence in your life that you are living under self-imposed legalism? If so, what remedy do you need to put in place?

Chapter 20 Resting

1. When do you rest? How does the way you rest communicate rest is holy?

2. Is your rest refreshing or do you find that physical rest is sabotaged because your soul is anxious?

3. Compose a list describing your plan for rest (use Nathan's list to get you started). Include things to do and things to think.

Chapter 21 Evaluations that Lead to Shame

1. Are there areas in your life that cause you to feel shame? Meditate on Psalm 34:5. How could this make a difference in your life?

2. Do you tend to compare yourself to others? What steps could you take to make God your standard of evaluation rather than others?

3. What reasons do you have to trust God?

4. Try following the bulleted steps on page 182 this week. Record the outcome.

Chapter 22 And When We Fail

1. What is your normal response to failure?

2. Review the bullet points on pages 186–87 describing the new character formed through suffering and endurance. Which of the traits are you beginning to see take shape in your life as a result of God's grace?

3. Try writing your own psalm praising the perfection of God.

Endnotes

1. Elyse Fitzpatrick, *Because He Loves Me* (Wheaton, IL: Crossway Books, 2008), 19.

2. Righteousness is the character or quality of being right or just (a) while perfection denotes a completeness and maturity in which any shortcomings or defects have been eliminated or left behind (b). (a) W. E. Vine, *Vine's Expository Dictionary,* Old Testament edited by F. F. Bruce (Old Tappan, NJ: Fleming H. Revell Company, 1981). (b) D. R. W. Wood, *New Bible Dictionary* (Downers Grove, IL: Intervarsity Press, 1996).

3. Robert Lowry, "Nothing but the Blood," *Gospel Music*, William Doane and Robert Lowry (New York: Biglow & Main, 1876).

4. People are defiled by sin. The Old Testament and the Gospels are filled with people who were ritually unclean and were not to be touched or associated with. The commandments for ceremonial washings and such foreshadow the cleansing power of the death of Jesus. Mark Driscoll and Gerry Breshears, *Death by Love* (Wheaton, IL: Crossway Books, 2008), 149.

5. To purify is to remove the defiling effect of sin. I. Howard Marshall, *The New International Commentary on the New Testament: The Epistles of John* (Grand Rapids, MI: William B. Eerdmans Publishing Company, 1978), 114.

6. Driscoll and Breshears, *Death by Love*, 154.

7. Throughout this book, the word *grace* will generally be used to speak of God's favor, help, and kindness directed to us through his Son.

8. Timothy S. Lane and Paul David Tripp, *How People Change* (Greensboro, NC: New Growth Press, 2008), 14.

9. John Calvin, *Institutes of the Christian Religion,* vol. 1, trans. Ford Lewis Battles (Philadelphia: Westminster Press, 1960) chap. XI, 8.

10. Michael Emlet, "Approaching Counselees as Saints, Sufferers, and Sinners," a session from the 2013 Faith Biblical Counseling Conference, Lafayette, IN. There is also a discussion of this in chapter 5 of Emlet's book *CrossTalk: Where Life and Scripture Meet* (Greensboro, NC: New Growth Press, 2012).

11. John MacArthur, *Matthew, 1–7, The MacArthur New Testament Commentary* (Chicago: Moody Press, 1985), 349–50.

12. John Piper and Justin Taylor, eds., *Suffering and the Sovereignty of God* (Wheaton, IL: Crossway Books, 2006).

13. Ruth Myers, *31 Days of Praise* (Sisters, OR: Multnomah Publishers, 1994), 12.

14. Jerry Bridges, *Trusting God: Even When Life Hurts* (Colorado Springs, CO: NavPress, 2008), 7.

15. Ibid.

16. Paul Tripp, "Working Your Way Up," accessed September 13, 2013, http://paultrippministries.blogspot.com/2006_11_19_archive.html.

17. Alfred Poirier, "The Cross and Criticism," *Journal of Biblical Counseling* 17, no. 3 (1999): 19.

18. Lyrics copied from *Timeless Truths Free Online Library*, http://library.timelesstruths.org/music/Rock_of_Ages/

19. John MacArthur, *Galatians* (Chicago: Moody Press, 1987), 61–62.

20. Ibid., 77–78. MacArthur goes on to explain that those who trust in the works of the Law are obligated to keep all things in the Law, without exception. This places them inevitably under a curse because no one has the ability to abide by everything the divine and perfect law of God demands. God's written law itself marks the danger of trying to live up to its standard, which is perfection. If you are relying on works of the law as your means of salvation, then you have to live by them perfectly. Perfection allows no exceptions, no failure of the smallest sort.

21. Phillip Keller, *A Shepherd Looks at Psalm 23* (Grand Rapids, MI: Zondervan, 1970).

22. Winston T. Smith, *Burned Out?* (Greensboro, NC: New Growth Press, 2006), 9.

23. David Powlison, *I'm Exhausted* (Greensboro, NC: New Growth Press, 2010), 19.

24. Testimony of a Vision of Hope graduate, used by permission. Vision of Hope is a residential treatment program for at-risk young women. It ministers to those struggling with addictions, habits of self-harm, eating disorders, and unplanned pregnancies.

With Grateful Thanks

To Jeff, my beloved husband, who encourages me not only with his words but with the example of his godly life and love for our Lord.

To Rob Green, who used the skills entrusted to him by God to read this manuscript, help me understand errors, and get to a better place.

To Steve Viars, for his wise leadership.

To the dear friends who have shared their lives with me in the perfectionism support group.

To many other writers and counselors who have led the way in helping me frame my thoughts on this topic.

To the staff at New Growth Press who have not only provided wise editing but have also become friends.

To all who have invested in my life, who have taught me about our marvelous God, and who have been examples of what a life redeemed by God looks like.